000232?

DATE DUE

OCT 0 1 1989	
APR 2 9 1992	
MAY 2 4 1994	
MAY 1 5 1995	

SAILING
TO WIN

SAILING TO WIN

by Bob Bavier

1983 Revised Edition

WITH 26 PHOTOGRAPHS
AND NUMEROUS LINE DRAWINGS

DODD, MEAD & COMPANY
New York

COPYRIGHT © 1947, 1948, 1951, 1962, 1965, 1969, 1973, 1978, 1983
By DODD, MEAD & COMPANY, Inc.
ALL RIGHTS RESERVED
NO PART OF THIS BOOK MAY BE REPRODUCED IN ANY FORM
WITHOUT PERMISSION IN WRITING FROM THE PUBLISHER
PRINTED IN THE UNITED STATES OF AMERICA

1   2   3   4   5   6   7   8   9   10

Library of Congress Cataloging in Publication Data

Bavier, Robert Newton, 1918–
Sailing to win.

1. Yacht racing.   2. Yacht racing—Rules.   I. Title.
GV826.5.B37   1983   797.1′4   82-22040
ISBN 0-396-08050-2

To

MY DAD

The Best Racing Skipper I Knew

Acknowledgments

It's hard to believe that thirty-six years have elapsed since this book was first published. Most of the principles of yacht racing remain the same, but techniques have changed. And I like to think I've learned something in all that time. Accordingly through the years new chapters have been added, some old ones modified. This current revision in 1983 brings the Racing Rules chapter up to date and modernizes other chapters.

Sincere thanks are extended to my fellow editors of *Yachting*, whose suggestions and editing of the manuscript have been of great help, to the U.S.Y.R.U. for permission to quote the racing rules and to Noroton Yacht Club for permission to duplicate its racing circular. I am especially grateful to Critchell Rimington, without whose encouragement the book would not have been undertaken; to W. H. and Dorothy deFontaine, who redrew my rough diagrams; to Stanley Rosenfeld, who helped select photographs from his vast collection; to the other marine photographers whose pictures help to update this edition; and to Walter C. Wood, who read the original manuscript and came up with some fine suggestions.

BOB BAVIER

Table of Contents

SAILING
TO WIN

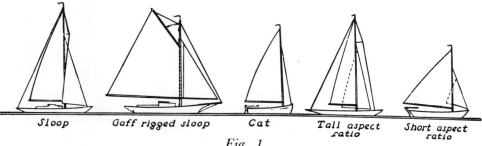

Sloop   *Gaff rigged sloop*   *Cat*   *Tall aspect ratio*   *Short aspect ratio*

Fig. 1

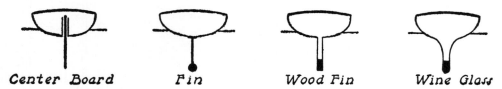

Center Board   *Fin*   *Wood Fin*   *Wine Glass*

Fig. 2—A centerboarder and three types of keel boats.

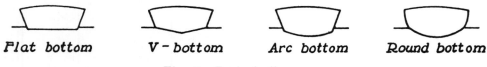

Flat bottom   *V - bottom*   *Arc bottom*   *Round bottom*

Fig. 3—Basic hull types.

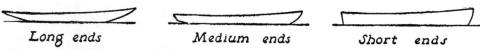

Long ends   *Medium ends*   *Short ends*

Fig. 4—Varying amounts of overhang. Long ends are suitable only for boats 30 feet or more over all and even then should not be excessive. As the boat's size diminishes, her ends should become proportionately shorter.

I

Let's Race Better

ARE YOU AN EXPERIENCED racing sailor who seldom wins and would like to do better? Are you a cruising and day sailing yachtsman who wants to get into racing? Or perhaps, are you about to buy your first boat and think racing would be the most fun?

In any case, I hope *Sailing to Win* will help you. Just writing it helped me because it got me thinking. Fortunately, you don't have to be a great brain to race successfully. But you do have to think, you do have to analyze your mistakes objectively and you do have to want to do better. A will to win helps because getting to the top in racing requires perseverance and attention to detail. A certain amount of natural ability is essential to be really good, but don't underestimate desire.

All I can hope to do in this book is point you in the right direction. The rest is up to you. Good luck and have fun.

What Boat to Buy?

If you are an old hand at racing you need no advice on what boat to buy. If you're a relative new-comer to racing, however, here are a few suggestions, and Figs. 1 through 4 opposite illustrate the various basic types of boats as well as some of the terms used to describe them. Don't rush out and buy the first boat that appeals to you. Find out first what fleets are popular in your locality, and find out too the level of competition in the different classes. Don't join a fleet where you will win all the time. Pretty soon winning won't mean much and you won't learn. Instead, join a fleet where the competition is at least as good as you are. And should you start winning regularly it is time to move to a hotter fleet. If you are a beginner you probably will want to avoid the more demanding types—the various Olympic classes. Still if you can take it, the fastest way to learn, the surest way to improve rapidly is to compete against experts.

3

Whatever boat you decide on, buy a good one of her type and buy good sails. There is nothing more discouraging than being beaten because of inferior equipment. And the extra you will pay at the outset will come back to you when you sell your boat. Unless you are very, very lucky *there are no bargains in boats*. If you can't afford a good boat of a certain type and good sails, get a good smaller boat or one in a less expensive class. And avoid secondhand sails, unless you want them purely for day sailing to save your racing suit. A suit of winning sails is seldom put on the market.

In buying an ocean racer it's even more important to avoid "bargains." Get a really good small one even though she costs as much as one considerably larger. The larger boat may be okay for cruising, but seldom for racing. An exception to the above *can* be if you buy a wooden boat. Fiberglass (and in the large boats, aluminum) is so popular now that good wooden boats are often underpriced. If she is well built and in top shape the maintenance won't be a great deal more. But be sure she is a good one, be sure to have her surveyed and also keep in mind that since you were able to buy her at a low price that's all you can expect to get when you sell. In general, by paying a little more you will get a lot more.

But enough of this general talk. Let's get on with what it takes to race well.

II

Tuning Your Racing Boat

FAST BOATS, well sailed, win races. Luck is also a factor though a small one, and it is a safe bet that the lucky skipper is also the smart one. Being smart, he realizes that no amount of good sailing will make a slow boat a winner in keen competition. Certain factors of design, briefly described in the previous chapter, determine whether a boat is potentially fast. But, no matter what her design, she becomes a dud against boats of the same or similar type unless she is placed and kept in proper racing trim. The process of getting a boat in this winning form is called tuning. Though we devote only one chapter to it, it is the groundwork without which one can never win consistently. Never underestimate its importance. You may be sure that your toughest competitors will not.

Tuning may be divided into two parts, tuning the hull and tuning the rig.

CONDITIONING AND TUNING THE HULL

Everything one does to the hull to make it faster (other than its original design) may be considered tuning. But, before doing anything to it, or to the rig, study your class rules and be sure that none of them is violated, either in spirit or in letter. Sharp practices sometimes win yacht races but never the respect of your competitors or crew. Some of the steps we shall outline here are outlawed in certain classes while in others they meet with full approval and are practiced by all of the better skippers.

The Importance of Smooth Bottoms and Topsides

There never was a class which outlawed the keeping of smooth bottoms and topsides and no single step in tuning a hull is of greater importance. Many

5

classes place restrictions on the number of times a boat may be hauled in a season but there is still no excuse for ever having anything but a smooth bottom. The slightest roughness on it, whether caused by seams that are squeezing, rough paint, slime, grass, or barnacles, will slow the boat down. Boats are generally pretty heavy and their weight must be supported by and driven through the water. Anyone who has taken a belly flopper from a high dive will attest to the fact that water is hard, that it can offer considerable resistance to an object attempting to pass through it. Designers work toward creating a form which will offer minimum resistance; it is up to you to create a surface on that form which will permit it to slide along as easily as possible. So we make the bottom smooth and the topsides also, knowing that much of the time they too are in contact with the water.

Obtaining a Smooth Surface

But how do we go about making a bottom smooth and keeping it so? A good, smooth paint job sufficiently thick to stand rubbing with wet-and-dry sandpaper (always used wet) and elbow grease supplies the principal answer. The decision whether to remove the paint or build upon the old paint will depend upon its condition. If the old paint has not flaked or chipped off in many spots and is smooth, it probably is advisable to repaint over it. The paint should be sanded thoroughly. Then the small imperfections should be glazed over with trowel cement or a thinner version of the same material of brushing consistency. In wooden boats it is essential that any bare spots be primed with paint before trying to use the trowel cement; otherwise the bare wood will soak up the oil in the cement and the cement will not adhere well. The same thing applies to putty. Trowel cement is far superior to any putty, even for large scratches and digs. Apply the cement in relatively thin layers. When it has hardened thoroughly, sand smooth with fine sandpaper. A perfectly smooth underbody can be built up in this way and if you have done a careful glazing job, it is often superior to a new paint job in appearance.

Should you find that the old paint chips off too easily to form a good under coat, it should be removed and a new surface built up. Prime the bare wood surface before trying to fill any of the small cracks or imperfections. Usually, suggestions as to the proper primer appear on a can of prepared paint. Gloss paints should in general have a flat undercoat or two while manufacturers of bottom paints usually recommend thinning the paint itself for the first coats. The hull should then be glazed wherever necessary as before. Never put trowel cement or other hardening putty in an open seam. Only non-hardening materials such as seam compound should be used to fill a planking seam. The excess material can then be removed after the seam has closed.

After the hull has been glazed, use fine sandpaper or garnet paper and in any event finish with the finest sandpaper, burlap or old carpet. In finishing, rub evenly with the grain of the planking and don't rub too hard. The fall, when the boat is hauled out, is a fine time for painting. After the surface has been properly prepared (and well dried out) apply a thin coat of bottom paint. Let it dry for a week and next week-end apply another. Two thin coats are far superior to one thick one.

Next spring, give her a final rub-down and then apply a last coat. When this is dry, many yachtsmen rub with steel wool or lightly with the finest sandpaper. For the ultimate it may then be finished by rubbing with a soft rag. Any amount of time spent on this preparation of the bottom will repay you later on.

Maintaining Fiberglass Hulls

The preparation and maintenance described above applies to wooden boats. In the case of fiberglass, the hull comes to you smooth as glass. Still it pays to sand it to make it even smoother and to produce a flat finish. If nicks occur in the gel coat, just apply new gel coat and sand smooth. If you get a deep gouge, mix up resin and glass fibers and fill the gouge. Then sand smooth, apply a gel coat and sand again. Numerous fiberglass repair kits are on the market and it's a cinch to use them.

If your fiberglass boat is kept in the water, a couple of coats of antifouling paint should be applied to the bottom over a fiberglass primer. Eventually, even with proper care, the topsides will fade and lose their sheen. This can be corrected by painting with epoxy paint. This won't be necessary for several years but will be eventually. These new paints are so hard that annual painting is unnecessary. At least once a season you should go over the topsides with fiberglass rubbing compound to remove stains and chalky deposits.

Maintenance of Aluminum Hulls

Although aluminum boats require little maintenance they should be painted both for appearance and protection. The most important thing to keep in mind, when using copper-bearing antifouling paint on the bottom, is to insure that there are sufficient barrier coats. Otherwise electrolitic action will set in between the copper bearing paint and the hull. If properly primed, however, this should never happen and aluminum boats will remain trouble free almost indefinitely.

What Kind of Paint?

In the past, white was the traditional color used on the topsides of boats. Black was about the only other color which found favor. Modern technology has produced fast colors and now we find a wide variety of semi-gloss and gloss enamels which are used extensively on small boats.

The original whites were of the soft, chalking variety which retain their white appearance by the slow erosion of the paint. This is still an excellent type of paint where the waters are dirty. Since it does not take colors very well, enamel paints are preferable where color is desired. In selecting colors for topsides, decks, etc., it is well to remember that darker colors, particularly black, dark grays, reds and greens absorb more light and are very hot. Seams in the topsides open more readily and, unless a similar color has been used for seam compound, any seam which was filled with white becomes an eyesore. The answer is to use soft pastel colors or tint your seam compound so that it blends with your topside color. The smoothest surface in the water is not the glossy shine of new paint but the carefully rubbed and burnished surface obtained by rubbing with water sandpaper, steel wool or pumice. Therefore, it is preferable to choose a semi-gloss rather than a high gloss paint. For white surfaces, many still prefer the soft chalking white both for appearance and for smoothness.

The new epoxy paints should be seriously considered. They are ideal on all but planked hulls and satisfactory also on hard glued planked hulls where the seams do not separate. These paints are harder to apply but last much longer.

Bottom Paints

The problem of selecting the proper bottom paint is not so much in obtaining a smooth surface as in keeping one. Marine growth of all kinds, grass, slime, and barnacles accumulate very quickly on a boat's bottom and in many places where the water is warm and brackish, growth can begin to form overnight on a boat. Even fresh water has its growths and a common enamel paint is seldom satisfactory. It is much better to buy a reliable marine paint made for the purpose. The cost of the best paint is cheap compared with a refinishing job if your experimental paint proves unsatisfactory. If you are not familiar with bottom paints, it is best to consult one of your experienced racing friends who will no doubt know of the best paints or types of paint for your particular locality. Often paints which are satisfactory for ocean salt water prove worthless further up in the bays or rivers where the warm brackish water presents an entirely different problem.

Without going into great detail, a general knowledge of bottom paints is essential to any racing skipper. In general there are two types of anti-fouling bottom paints, the soft or defoliating paints and the hard enamels. The first type not only has poisonous ingredients but erodes so that any marine growth that might attach itself to the paint eventually drops off. Such paint wears out by the end of the season or, if scrubbed frequently, it may come off in midseason and require repainting. It makes a smooth bottom but is not to be compared with a real polished bottom obtainable through use of one of the harder paints. It is particularly good for places where the boats foul up very quickly or for larger boats whose haulouts for cleaning can be costly.

Most small boat racing skippers prefer hard racing enamels which are only slightly anti-fouling in most localities and which can be rubbed with water sandpaper until they are like a fine piece of furniture. It has been found that light colored paints do not foul up as quickly as darker ones and also the psychological effect of being able to see the slime and growth makes one keep the boat cleaner than when the slime is camouflaged against a dark color. Good bottom enamels are available even in white. There are several bronze paints that harden and polish like sheet copper when rubbed with steel wool. With some bottom paints the boat should be launched soon after application. Read the directions!

Cleaning the Bottom of the Boat in the Water

All hard bottom paints require frequent cleaning, but this is not a difficult job since most small boats need not be hauled for bottom cleaning. There are several methods which may be utilized. One is to haul the boat down slightly with the jib halliard at the float and clean with a long handled scrub brush from a dinghy. This is especially effective with round bottom boats and it is not necessary to have the whole bottom out of water. In fact, with brushes and water sandpaper, the cleaning can often be done better under water than with the bottom dry in the air. One can go overboard at the mooring and scrub with a brush, following up with wet-or-dry sandpaper and a piece of toweling. Work gloves, which come with a turkish towel-like surface are fine for a finishing rub and locate spots which the brush has missed, such as the area between keel and rudder.

Flat or arc bottom boats are particularly easy to keep clean. The trick here is to make a cleaning paddle like the one developed by my friend Walter C.

("Jack") Wood. It consists of a 1″ × 6″ × 12″ board attached to a 1″ × 2″ × 5′ handle. The top surface of this is covered with several layers of stiff bristle carpet carried over the edges of the board and tacked underneath. A rectangle of life preserver cork is then screwed over the under side after being notched to fit over the handle. This board has a great amount of flotation and it is only necessary to run it under the boat and work it back and forth. The flotation presses it hard against the bottom and little effort is required to use it. It is best to have someone sit on the opposite side of your boat while cleaning so that your own weight is counterbalanced. To get the keel clean, and to insure that no spots have been missed, it is advisable to finish up by going overboard and swimming under the boat. The swimmer will find a mask or goggles handy.

Shaping Centerboard and Rudder

Getting a smooth finish isn't the whole story. Unless class rules prevent it, extra speed can be gained by planing or filing the leading and trailing edges of the rudder and centerboard. The trailing edge should be made particularly fine.

A frequent fault in centerboard boats is a board which does not fit snugly in the trunk. When lowered, boards often wobble, especially as the boat increases speed. A chattering board of this sort is a serious drag. Even if it does not actually wobble, unless it fits snugly it tends to twist in its slot and must be forced through the water at an angle instead of in a true fore and aft line. When a centerboard boat goes faster on one tack than on the other, or when the board can be felt to rattle and vibrate in its slot, a refitting job is in order. It is simple to add a bit of wood to narrow the slot and insure a snug fit and it is well worth the slight effort involved.

In keel boats, make sure that the forward side of the keel is free from gouges or other irregularities. Mooring cables, submerged logs, etc., sometimes come in contact with the keel and can easily roughen it.

Lighten the Hull

Another cardinal rule in tuning the hull is to make it light. It should be built as light as is practicable and as class rules permit. In wooden boats not only should planking be thin, it should also be of light wood, either cedar or mahogany, never teak.

Generally, however, the boat builder decides on the kind and thickness of wood he will use and the sailor takes her as is (which is fortunate since builders seldom go too far in the direction of lightness whereas some skippers might, if given a free hand).

Often, a hull can be lightened or at least kept light after it has been delivered. Perhaps floor boards are heavier than need be and can be planed down. In some classes they are even removed, but it is our opinion that this is going too far. Sometimes an extra seat or unnecessary locker can be taken out to advantage.

Old boats often accumulate a great many coats of deck paint. If yours has, getting rid of them by paint remover or burning will remove many unnecessary pounds from above the water line where they are most harmful. When repainting, two coats should be plenty. Try one of the nonskid types of deck paint which enable the crew to work faster and with less chance of slipping overboard.

The fittings which are attached to the hull can often be lightened and located to better advantage. Place halliard winches as low down as possible, preferably right next to the floor boards. But never remove necessary fittings or reduce the efficiency of those you have by relocating them.

Excess gear and sails should be left ashore. Retain all that is really necessary but don't allow your boat to become a catchall for equipment which is not vital. An anchor should be carried but, if you are racing, take a lighter one than would be used for cruising. The anchor line can be light, too. By saving a few pounds here and a few more there, it isn't long before you have reduced the weight considerably. Weight of the crew is relatively unimportant because this is live ballast which can move to the position in the boat where it will be most helpful. It is wise, however, not to have your crew exceed in number those required to handle the boat to best efficiency.

Keeping the Hull Light

Getting a hull light isn't the whole story. It is important to keep her so. In classes which so permit, if your boat is made of wood, hauling her out after every race prevents the wood in the hull from soaking up water and helps retain its original lightness. In all classes it is vital to keep the boat dry inside. Always sponge out the last drop of water before a race and keep her dry during the race. Water sloshing around can do much to make a boat sluggish. Since even a wood boat will leak hardly at all in a week's time, it is wise to bail her dry before leaving her after the race and then place a tent over the cockpit to keep rainwater out. She will then stay reasonably dry inside during the week and any water which the hull soaks up will be from the outside alone. Remember, it is the sum total of a number of small, apparently inconsequential attentions which make a boat faster than her competitors.

The Importance of Trim

Far more important than the total weight a boat carries is locating that weight in the correct position. The boat must be kept in proper trim. If too much gear or too many crew members are aft in the cockpit, she will be down by the stern. She no longer assumes the lines her designer intended and will drag. Also, balance is apt to be affected and she may steer poorly. The same is true if too much weight is forward. So distribute your weights as evenly as possible, keeping them near the center. A good rule is to have the boat in the same trim after crew and equipment are on board as she was when light. Some boats sail better if slightly down by the bow and a very few if a bit down by the stern. But these are unusual characteristics. In any event, once you have determined her fastest fore and aft trim, make sure to locate your movable weight so that she retains that trim.

Athwartships trim is more a matter of sailing than of tuning and will be discussed in later chapters.

TUNING THE RIG

Important as it is to have a properly conditioned hull, it is perhaps even more important to tune the rig. One of the basic principles of proper tuning is to make the boat balance so that she answers her helm easily with only slight pressure on the tiller. Weight distribution plays a part in achieving balance, as does the position of the centerboard, but both are secondary to the proper positioning of the spars. In light airs, the average boat should have no helm. If the tiller is let go, the boat should tend to hold her course. As the wind increases, she should have a slight tendency to round up into the wind. But the helmsman should never be forced to tug on the tiller to keep her off. If such is necessary, the rudder will be at an angle to the boat's line of advance and the boat will be forced to pull it protestingly through the water. That hardly makes for speed.

Proper Raking of the Mast

To achieve balance, one of the first steps is to rake the mast properly. Masts are usually set either straight up and down or raking slightly aft. On rare occasions a forward rake is effective, but more often a pronounced rake aft works best. If the boat has a lee helm, try raking the mast aft more. If she

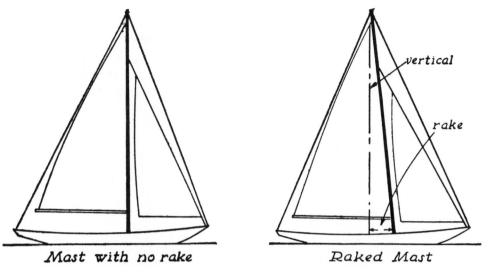

Mast with no rake   Raked Mast

Fig. 5—The correct amount of rake is essential for balance.

has an excessive weather helm, reduce the amount of rake (or even try raking
it forward) until better balance is achieved. (Fig. 5).

There may be times when this procedure fails to produce the expected
results. I remember Jack Wood once told me of a boat of his which increased
her weather helm as the mast was raked forward. The explanation appears to
have been contained in the fact that this particular boat had a boom which
hung very low aft. Consequently, when the boat heeled, the weather side of
the boat sheltered the lower leech and foot of the sail. Raising the sail got it up
into the wind where its effect more than offset the shift of center of sail area.
The remedy, in this case, was either to sheet the main down off the quarter to
relieve the leech pressure, or to move the whole mast forward.

The mast should have only a slight curve fore and aft and it should *never*
curve forward. As the breeze increases, it is often advisable to put more curve
in the mast. This tends to flatten the sail because it pulls the luff forward.
Since the flatter sail is more efficient in strong winds, greater speed is the
usual result. As the wind lessens, reduce the curve or remove it altogether.
Curving is done by easing the headstay (if there is one), taking an increased
strain on the backstay and adjusting the position of the heel of the mast.
Pulling the foot of the mast aft, and/or placing it further forward at the deck,
tends to force the upper part forward. Since backstays prevent it from going
forward, a curve results. (Fig. 6). A powerful boom vang can also induce
curvature.

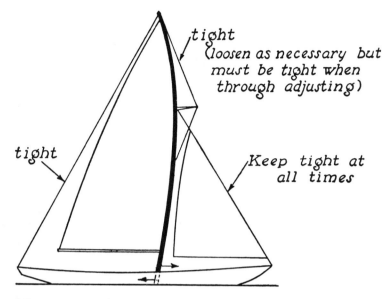

Fig. 6—Methods of curving the mast.

Adjusting Shrouds

It is important to guard against any sidewise curve. A mast should be as straight as possible. To achieve this, it is best to make the upper shrouds (those leading to the upper part of the mast) taut and the lower ones somewhat slack. The upper ones, being longer, will stretch more than the shorter lowers. Hence, if the lowers are equally taut, a sidewise curve is unavoidable. In ¾ or ⅞ rigs, however, where the jibstay does not go to the masthead, the lower shrouds, particularly the after lowers if the lowers are doubled, should be nearly as taut as the upper shrouds. Making them taut keeps the jibstay from sagging, and a straight jibstay is essential for upwind speed, especially in heavy air. (Fig. 7A and 7B). It is usually better to have the whole mast *leaning* sidewise slightly than to have it *curving* sidewise. Some boats go well with the top of the mast sagging to leeward, but this is unusual.

Spreaders should be cocked upward so that the angles between the spreader and the shroud passing over it are the same or nearly the same both above and below the spreader.

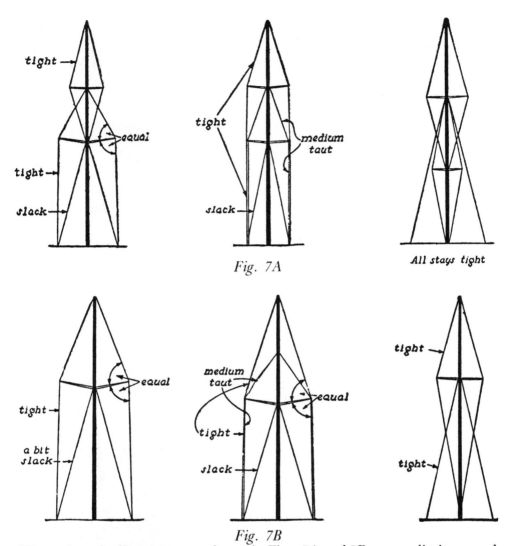

Fig. 7A

All stays tight

Fig. 7B

These shroud adjustments, as shown in Figs. 7A and 7B, are preliminary and should be followed by final tuning to insure straightness.

Preliminary adjustments should be made at anchor and then, after the boat is under sail, sight up along the mast track to see how it stands. Adjust the turnbuckles to correct and sight again, repeating the process until the mast is straight. Be careful not to over-tauten. Loosening the lowers can often accomplish more than over-tautening the uppers. If shrouds are made too taut the mast has added compression stress, is more apt to break, and is prone to bow into worse curves than existed before adjusting began. (Fig. 8). Don't make shrouds too taut! When you think you have the mast straight, take pictures of your boat under sail. Then sight along the mast in the picture and, like as not, you will find a curve still exists which you might be able to remove.

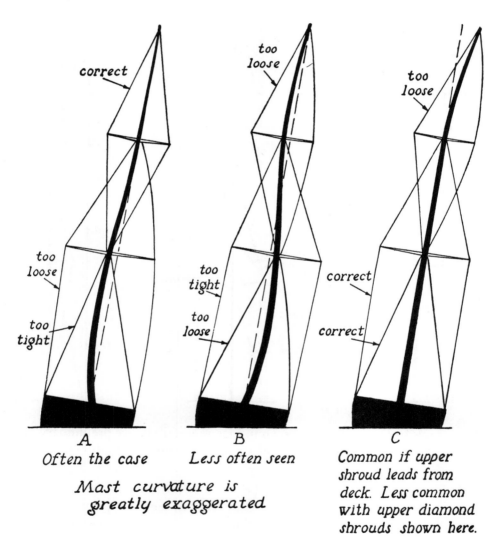

Fig. 8—Results of faulty shroud adjustment.

Keep the Jibstay Taut

While the shrouds should often be a bit loose, jibstays and backstays must be taut. A loose jibstay will curve off to leeward and will slow the boat down, especially while beating to windward, so set the jibstay up taut. And, to keep the mast from raking forward, backstays must be made taut also. As a general rule, taut stays and not quite so taut shrouds is a good axiom. On a reach or a run, however, both backstay and jibstay should be eased. This will give more draft to the sails, and on these points of sailing it doesn't hurt to have the jibstay sagging a bit to leeward. The same can apply in light air even when beating to windward. (See Fig. 9 for principles of stay adjustment).

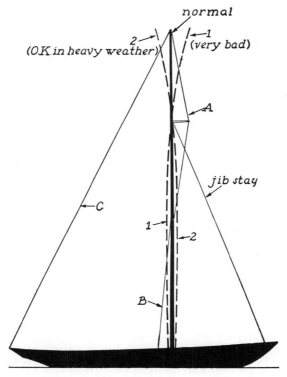

Condition 1 — A and B too tight; C too loose
Condition 2 — A and B loose; C tight
(may be desirable in heavy weather)

Fig. 9—Cause and effect of stay adjustment.

Hoisting Sails Properly

In a later chapter, we will go into the proper care and setting of sails at some length. It is worth mentioning now, however, that a good tuning job can be nullified by sails that are poorly hoisted. Hoist them reasonably taut and as they stretch keep taking in the slack, preferably by means of a downhaul or cunningham to pull the foot down rather than attempting to hoist further.

With the sail full of wind, it may be possible to hoist it further and it may be damaged or pulled out of shape in the attempt. With a downhaul, it is easy to tack down both main and jib, either during a tack or by luffing slightly. It is especially important to see that the jib is hoisted tightly and that there is no bow between hanks on the stay. In light air, a slack luff on the main may increase the sail's draft and thereby make it faster. The same is true of the jib. Nowadays almost all jibs have stretchy luffs. As wind increases, halliard tension should also be increased. This not only flattens the draft to make the jib more effective, but also reduces the backwind into the mainsail. When you are sailing downwind, however, be sure to ease halliard tension.

The main boom outhaul should also be kept well pulled out (except in light airs). Avoid pulling it too hard, but always hard enough to make a smoothly setting sail. Often a hard spot or a hooking leech can be removed by varying the tension on luff and foot. Try it.

Sheet Leads

Sails will certainly set poorly unless the sheet leads are in the right position. On loose-footed jibs, the sheet should follow approximately in the direction of the mitre line. A better rule is to watch where your jib luffs. If the head luffs sooner than the foot (the most common case) the lead is too far aft. Place it further forward until both head and foot luff simultaneously. When this happens the lead is correctly located. If the lower part of the luff breaks first, the sheet is led too far forward. Move it aft to correct. (Fig. 10).

Main sheets should be led to a position on deck which facilitates trim. Often it is advisable to lead the hauling part from the middle of the boom. This prevents the boom from curving upward and thus helps to retain the sail's shape. In pliable booms, it bows the boom downward as the breeze increases, thereby flattening the sail. Since a sail with less draft goes faster in a breeze, this downward bend is desirable.

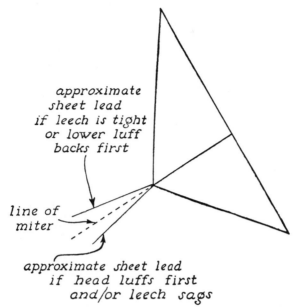

approximate
sheet lead
if leech is tight
or lower luff
backs first

line of
miter

approximate sheet lead
if head luffs first
and/or leech sags

Fig. 10—The lower lead shown here is more often correct.

Traveller Adjustments

The position of the main traveller is vital for speed. In light air the traveller should be trimmed to windward of the centerline. This permits the main
sheet to be eased to increase draft and give more drive, without the boom
sagging off to leeward so far that pointing ability is sacrificed. As the wind
increases the traveller should be eased farther to leeward. In a strong breeze
this enables the boat to be sailed more on her feet, and by trimming the main
sheet very hard you will still be able to point.

In very strong air there is an alternate way of keeping the boat from
heeling too far. By keeping the traveller amidships or even to windward, you
can ease the main sheet and wind will be spilled from the top part of the main,
with only the lower part providing drive. Since the traveller is to windward
the boom won't be so far to leeward that you can't point.

On most boats in heavy air it is more effective to ease the traveller well to
leeward and trim the main hard. But the alternative method is worth a try. It
works well on some boats and in some conditions.

Reduce Weight and Windage Aloft

Among the very basic rules of tuning are the reduction of weight and windage aloft. Saving a pound on the mast is the equivalent of many, many pounds saved in the weight of the hull. *One pound* taken from the top of a small boat's mast can effect a noticeable increase in her stability and speed.

Make Spars Light

The first step in saving weight aloft is to make spars light. Hollow spars are far stronger for a given weight than solid ones. Sitka spruce, being both light and strong, is recommended as the choice wood for spars but aluminum spars are better than the finest wooden ones. Light spars are subject to bowing from the compression exerted by shrouds and halliards pulling down. Part of this pull can be removed by installing a halliard hook. This is a device at the top of the mast which holds the sail up after it has been hoisted and permits the halliard to be slacked.

Weight can be further reduced by having light rigging, strong enough to hold the mast with a sufficient margin of safety, *but no stronger*. Most boats have standing rigging that is too heavy. Neat terminals to the rigging save both weight and windage. Truloc fittings are a good substitute for the more bulky splices, which are seldom used anymore. The saving in windage is just as important as the reduction in weight. Masts and fittings offer resistance to the wind and tend to push the boat backwards when beating into it. Any amount of streamlining or reduction in size that can be applied to the mast (making it pear shaped, for example), rigging, spreaders, and fittings is all to the good.

Lightness can be achieved in spar fittings by the use of aluminum alloys. Micarta sheaves are both light and strong. Stainless steel is best for tangs and masthead fittings. Being strong they can be made small and compact to start with and then by filing, drilling and turning on a lathe one can often reduce the dimensions of their stronger parts. Well designed mast hardware should be strong enough to save a comfortable safety margin but no part of it should be stronger than its weakest link. Reducing the weight of the heavier, stronger parts reduces weight without incurring risk. But be sure that you know what you are about.

A masthead fly or pennant is useful but it should be light. The light ones (2 to 4 ounces) work best and if they save a few ounces at the top of the mast they become an even greater asset.

Keep Weights Low

Reducing the weight of mast fittings isn't the whole story. Keeping them as low down as possible is an equally valuable contribution to the boat's stability. If possible, move halliard winches below decks or at least get them as low as possible. If you can, put turnbuckles below, also, and lead the shrouds through the deck. Both of these steps not only move the weight down but also reduce windage.

Rigging Should Be Kept as Simple as Possible

Simplicity should be the aim of the rig's design. Have as many spreaders, shrouds and stays as are required to keep the mast straight, or reasonably straight, but no more. The smaller the boat, the fewer the fittings required; some boats make the error of duplicating the rig designs of boats considerably larger.

Simplifying the rig will reduce windage. Remove lazy jacks and topping lifts. They have no place in small racing boats. If possible, lead halliards inside the mast. If this cannot be done, much of the effect can be gained by leading them down the forward side of the mast through small fairleads rather than allowing them to flank the spar.

Both weight and windage aloft can be reduced by bending light line onto the end of the spinnaker halliard. This messenger will be much lighter and far less bulky than the halliard itself. On windward legs, lower the halliard and have only the messenger up. As the weather mark is neared, the spinnaker halliard can be hoisted and made ready for use. Make all halliards light. They have only slight strain once the sail is hoisted and it is best to have a light one which needs replacement as soon as it shows wear than one that is too comfortably stout.

Make the Rig Work

In our zeal to reduce weight and windage, we must never lessen the working qualities of the rig. Sheaves for halliards and sheet blocks should be of large diameter. Running rigging passes over them much more easily. And, in the case of the wire halliard sheave, a large one causes less wire fatigue. A small sheave causes the wire to make a sharp bend, invites failure and may make the wire spiral like a spring. Furthermore, running rigging should *run*.

Big, well-oiled sheaves assist this and pliable sheets and halliards are the next step. Dacron sheets will pay real dividends, as will stainless steel wire for halliards. Don't make sheets too light, however. They must be large enough to permit a good hand-hold. Avoiding tangles by keeping halliards and sheets neatly coiled will go far to insure that they are ready to run easily and quickly. Winches, though they add weight, will more than repay the extra poundage by the greater efficiency which results. A large jib sheet winch is a big help when it comes to trimming the jib properly and fast. The same can be said of winches for the main sheet or halliards. Jigs are often a satisfactory substitute for winches. Taping over turnbuckle cotter pins may add a few ounces of weight but by all means do it. If you can thereby save a sail from being ripped as it brushes against them minutes may be saved, not to mention the expense of repairing the rip.

In short, spend hours getting a smooth finish on topsides and bottom, lighten the hull, reduce weight and windage aloft, but never reduce the working efficiency of your boat and her rig unless the end justifies it. Even then, be cautious. But remember that in tuning a boat it is the sum total of all the little things you do which makes her fast. No matter how unimportant each separate step might appear, it is worth doing. It takes time and care but you will like the result.

III

The New Racing Rules

T<small>RY TO</small> <small>IMAGINE</small> a football game in which one team neither knew the rules nor cared to abide by them. The result might be rough and exciting, but hardly scientific or a fair test of skill. It would be tough on the team that was attempting to follow the rules and yet, if the officials were on the job, the rule breaking team would be almost sure to lose.

It makes just about as much sense to attempt to race a sailboat without understanding and abiding by the rules. If you don't, it is hard not only on your competitors but on yourself, too. You are almost certain to be disqualified. Don't start without knowing the rules, not by heart, but better than that. Know them instinctively. It is really quite easy, particularly under the new set of rules adopted in 1981 and frozen without change until 1985. The really significant parts of the new rules, and the only ones which require discussion, are Fundamental Rule, Fair Sailing, Part I, Definitions, and Part IV, Right of Way Rules. The other parts of the new rules have to do with Sailing Rules Other Than Right of Way, Signals, Management of Races, General Requirements, and Protests, Disqualifications and Appeals. They serve as useful background information and for use as reference and should be read by all racing skippers carefully enough to get a working knowledge of all. But, because they are easy to understand, they need not concern us here. The full set of rules can be purchased from the office of the U.S.Y.R.U., P.O. Box 209, Newport, Rhode Island 02840, for $5.00.

A casual knowledge of Parts I and IV, however, is not sufficient. The skipper should know instantly and almost instinctively whether or not his yacht has right of way. In the excitement of a tight race there is not time to ponder the rules. Instead a mental picture of the rule which has application in the existing situation must leap to mind. Instinctive knowledge of this sort will not only prevent disqualification but will insure that no distance is lost while attempting to determine one's rights. If even half a boat length can be gained by knowing at once which rule applies, your complete knowledge of that rule will have been well worth while. Races are won by gaining a few feet here and a few more there until finally a winning margin is built up.

In discussing the new racing rules, after the Fundamental Rule we will next consider the definitions so that when we come to the right of way rules the terms used will make sense. The definitions and rules will be indented to differentiate them from any comment which might accompany them.

FUNDAMENTAL RULES

Fair Sailing

> A yacht shall participate in a race or series of races in an event only by fair sailing, superior speed and skill, and, except in team races, by individual effort. However, a yacht may be disqualified under this rule only in the case of a clear-cut violation of the above principles and only when no other rule applies.

This rule used to be in Part V but is given added importance by leading off the rules. It is seldom enforced and should never be used as a cop-out by protest committees who feel a yacht is wrong but unable to find a rule which applies. But if a sailor is found to be guilty of gross poor sportsmanship or of cheating, here is the rule to nail him on. It's been applied several times in recent years and is proving effective in keeping the sport clean.

Responsibility of a Yacht

> It shall be the sole responsibility of each yacht to decide whether or not to start or to continue to race.

This rule is intended partly to get race organizers or committees off the hook from possible lawsuits in the event a killer storm springs up after the start. It is intended even more to try to make all sailors realize that the responsibility is really theirs, and that they must exercise good judgment. It is more than coincidence that this rule was added after the 1979 Fastnet Race that took so many lives.

PART 1: DEFINITIONS

Racing

> A yacht is *racing* from her preparatory signal until she has either *finished* and cleared the finishing line and finishing *marks* or retired, or until the race has been *postponed*, *abandoned* or *cancelled*, or a general recall has been signalled, except that in match or team races, the sailing in-structions may prescribe that a yacht is *racing* from any specified time before the preparatory signal.

The most important point here is that you can be disqualified before the start and after the finish. Also, if in the vicinity of the start after the preparatory signal, it is then too late to decide not to start. You are already racing and will be given a DNF if you don't start and complete the course. Note the special provision for match and team racing.

Starting

A yacht *starts* when, after fulfilling her penalty obligations, if any, under rule 51.1(c), Sailing the Course, and after her starting signal, any part of her hull, crew or equipment first crosses the starting line in the direction of the course to the first *mark*.

Finishing

A yacht *finishes* when any part of her hull, or of her crew or equipment in normal position, crosses the finishing line from the direction of the course from the last *mark*, after fulfilling her penalty obligations, if any, under rule 52.2, Touching a Mark.

Luffing

Altering course towards the wind.

Note that there is no need for sails to be shaking in order for a boat to be luffing under the definition.

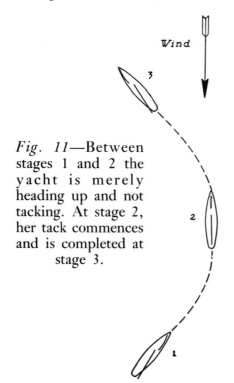

Fig. 11—Between stages 1 and 2 the yacht is merely heading up and not tacking. At stage 2, her tack commences and is completed at stage 3.

Tacking

A yacht is tacking from the moment she is beyond head to wind until she has *borne away* when beating to windward, to a *close-hauled* course; if not beating to windward, to the course on which her mainsail has filled.

It is important to notice that a yacht has not begun to tack until after she is beyond head to wind. See Fig. 11. Notice that there is a similar provision as regards gybing. Prior to tacking a yacht is luffing and prior to jibing she is bearing away.

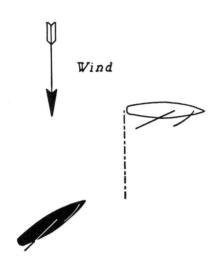

Fig. 12—Black is clear astern of White because she is aft of a line projected abeam from White's aftermost point.

Bearing Away

Altering course away from the wind until a yacht begins to *jibe*.

Jibing

A yacht begins to *jibe* at the moment when, with the wind aft, the foot of her mainsail crosses her center line and completes the *jibe* when the mainsail has filled on the other *tack*.

On a Tack

A yacht is on a tack except when she is *tacking* or *jibing*. A yacht is on the *tack (starboard* or *port)* corresponding to her *windward* side.

Remember that the windward side is the opposite side from that on which the main boom is carried. Hence with the boom to port the yacht is on the starboard tack.

Close-hauled

A yacht is *close-hauled* when sailing by the wind as close as she can lie with advantage in working to windward.

Clear Astern and Clear Ahead; Overlap

A yacht is *clear astern* of another when her hull and equipment in normal position are abaft an imaginary line projected abeam from the aftermost point of the other's hull and equipment in normal position. The other yacht is *clear ahead*.

The yachts *overlap* when neither is *clear astern;* or when, although one is *clear astern*, an intervening yacht *overlaps* both of them.

The terms *clear astern, clear ahead* and *overlap* apply to yachts on opposite *tacks* only when they are subject to rule 42 (Rounding or Passing Marks and Obstructions).

Notice that in interpreting this definition the sails, booms, bowsprits, etc., of the yachts involved, not only the hulls, must not overlap if a yacht is to be considered clear astern. See Fig. 12. Note also that two yachts which *in themselves* are not overlapped are considered overlapped when an intervening yacht overlaps both of them. See Fig. 13.

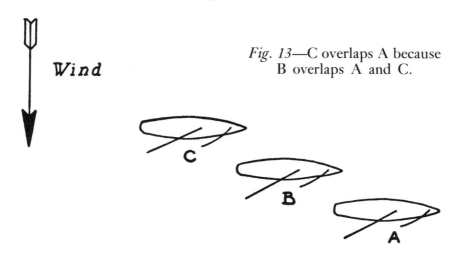

Wind

Fig. 13—C overlaps A because B overlaps A and C.

Leeward and Windward

The *leeward* side of a yacht is that on which she is, or, when head to wind, was, carrying her mainsail. The opposite side is the *windward* side.

When neither of two yachts on the same tack is *clear astern*, the one on the *leeward* side of the other is the *leeward yacht*. The other is the *windward yacht*. See Fig. 14.

Proper Course

A *proper course* is any course which a yacht might sail after the starting signal, in the absence of the other yacht or yachts affected, to *finish* as quickly as possible. The course sailed before *luffing* or *bearing away* is presumably, but not necessarily, that yacht's *proper course*. There is no *proper course* before the starting signal.

This is one of the few instances in the new rules where the facts of the situation are difficult to determine. Sometimes it may be hard to prove what is and what is not a proper course. Any course, however, which obviously results in completing the course in slow time could not be considered proper.

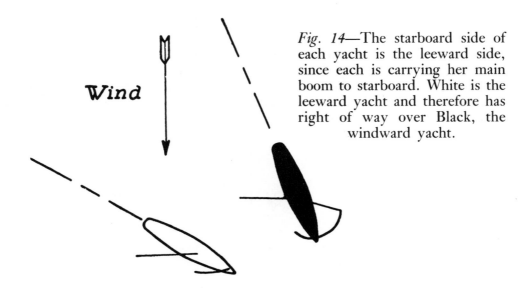

Fig. 14—The starboard side of each yacht is the leeward side, since each is carrying her main boom to starboard. White is the leeward yacht and therefore has right of way over Black, the windward yacht.

In practice, it will usually be possible to tell when a boat is not sailing a proper course, but remember that one can deviate from the direct line to the next mark (to get a stronger wind or better slant or in tacking down wind, for example) and still sail a proper course.

Mark

A *mark* is any object specified in the sailing instructions which a yacht must round or pass on a required side.

Every ordinary part of a *mark* ranks as part of it, including a flag, flagpole, boom or hoisted boat, but excluding ground tackle and any object either accidentally or temporarily attached to the *mark*.

Notice particularly that not only the buoys which are to be rounded to complete the course, but also all government buoys which the instructions indicate must be passed on a specified side are considered marks of the course.

Obstruction

An *obstruction* is any object, including a vessel under way, large enough to require a yacht, when more than one overall length away from it, to make a substantial alteration of course to pass on one side or the other, or any object which can be passed on one side only, including a buoy when the yacht in question cannot safely pass between it and the shoal or object which it marks.

Don't be confused by this one. A yacht can be several lengths or less than a length from an object and still have said object rank as an obstruction (or not so rank). The distance referred to in the definition is merely a clever way of determining how big an object must be (in relation to the yachts racing) in order to rank as an obstruction.

Postponement

A *postponed* race is one which is not started at its scheduled time and which can be sailed at any time the race committee may decide.

Abandonment

An *abandoned* race is one which the race committee declares void at any time after the starting signal, and which can be resailed at its discretion.

Cancellation

A *cancelled* race is one which the race committee decides will not be sailed thereafter.

PART IV: RIGHT OF WAY RULES

Assuming that the foregoing definitions are thoroughly understood, we are now ready to consider Part IV, Right of Way Rules. Any racing skipper must know all of these but the problem is simplified by the fact that there are two basic rules which apply in the vast majority of racing situations. These basic rules are: a) If two yachts are on opposite tacks the port tack yacht shall keep clear, and b) If they are on the same tack the windward yacht must keep clear. While these two rules apply in the vast majority of cases, they are far from the full story and in fact there are a few instances, fortunately only a very few, in which they do not apply.

All Right of Way Rules apply as indicated by the following paragraph which is included in the rule book as an introduction to Part IV.

Rights and Obligations when Yachts Meet

The rules of Part IV do not apply in any way to a vessel which is neither intending to *race* nor *racing*; such vessel shall be treated in accordance with the International Regulations for Preventing Collisions at Sea or Government Right of Way Rules applicable in the area concerned.

The rules of Part IV apply only between yachts which either are intending to *race* or are *racing* in the same or different races, and, except when rule 3.2(b)(xxviii) (Race Continues After Sunset) applies, replace the International Regulations for Preventing Collisions at Sea or Government Right of Way Rules applicable to the area concerned, from the time a yacht intending to *race* begins to sail about in the vicinity of the starting line until she has either *finished* or retired and has left the vicinity of the course.

Part IV is divided into three sections, A through C. Hereafter the sections and the rules under each will be considered in the order in which they are listed. The first two rules (31, 32) are self explanatory and hence are merely quoted.

SECTION A

31. Disqualification

31.1. A yacht may be disqualified or otherwise penalized for infringing a rule of Part IV only when the infringement occurs while she is *racing*, whether or not a collision results.

31.2. A yacht may be disqualified before or after she is racing for seriously hindering a yacht which is *racing*, or for infringing the sailing instructions.

32. Avoiding Collisions

A right-of-way yacht which fails to make a reasonable attempt to avoid a collision resulting in serious damage may be disqualified as well as the other yacht.

33. Rule Infringement

33.1. *Accepting Penalty*—A yacht which realizes she has infringed a racing rule or a sailing instruction is under an obligation either to retire promptly or to exonerate herself by accepting an alternative penalty when so prescribed in the sailing instructions, but when she does not retire or exonerate herself and persists in *racing*, other yachts shall continue to accord her such rights as she has under the rules of Part IV.

33.2. *Contact Between Yachts Racing*—When there is contact between the hull, equipment or crew of two yachts, both shall be disqualified or otherwise penalized unless:
either
(a)   one of the yachts retires in acknowledgement of the infringement, or exonerates herself by accepting an alternative penalty when so prescribed in the sailing instructions, or

(b)   one or both of these yachts acts in accordance with rule 68 (Protests by Yachts).

33.3. *Waiving Rule 33.2*—A race committee acting under rule 33.2 may waive the requirements of the rule when it is satisfied that the contact was minor and unavoidable.

Rule 33.2 is one of the most unpopular of all the rules. There are occasions such as on a crowded starting line when two yachts, despite their best efforts to keep clear, do make minor contact. It could even be so minor as the crew of the leeward yacht hiking far out and having his head barely touch the main of the boat to windward. Many sailors feel that in such accidental contact and when neither skipper was trying to gain an unfair advantage, it is only fair and sporting not to lodge a protest. But the rule says otherwise and unless one retires *both* can be disqualified if neither protests. Should the two skippers hail each other and agree that the incident was so minor as to best be forgotten, that still doesn't insure that they won't be thrown out. Rule 68.1 gives a third yacht witnessing the incident the right to protest. Hence the only safe recourse when contact is made is to protest if you feel you were right. Whether you like this rule or not, it demonstrates the peril of being a good sport and suggesting that a minor unavoidable contact be overlooked. The purpose of the rule, of course, is to encourage observance of the rules. But still, most sailors don't like it.

Rule 33.3 does give the race committee an out on the obligation to disqualify both yachts, but only if they find that contact was minor and unavoidable.

34. *Hailing*

34.1. Except when *luffing* under rule 38.1 (Luffing and Sailing above a Proper Course after Starting), a right-of-way yacht which does not hail before or when making an alteration of course which may not be foreseen by the other yacht may be disqualified as well as the yacht required to keep clear when a collision resulting in serious damage occurs.

34.2. A yacht which hails when claiming the establishment or termination of an *overlap* or insufficiency of room at a *mark* or *obstruction* thereby helps to support her claim for the purposes of rule 42 (Rounding or Passing Marks and Obstructions).

SECTION B—PRINCIPAL RIGHT OF WAY RULES AND THEIR LIMITATIONS

These rules apply except when over-ridden by a rule in Section C.

35.*Limitations on Altering Course*

When one yacht is required to keep clear of another, the right-of-way yacht shall not so alter course as to prevent the other yacht from keeping clear; or so as to obstruct her while she is keeping clear, except:

(a)   to the extent permitted by rule 38.1 (Same Tack, Luffing and Sailing above a Proper Course after Starting), and

(b)   when assuming a *proper* course:
either
    (i)   to *start*, unless subject to rule 40 (Same Tack, Luffing before Starting), or to the second part of rule 44.1(b) (Returning to Start), or
    (ii)   when rounding a *mark*.

A typical violation of this rule on the part of a starboard tack close-hauled yacht would be bearing off below a full and by course in order to trick a port tack yacht into believing she could cross safely and then, at the last instant, resuming a normal close-hauled course. If this action resulted in a collision or necessitated a subsequent alteration of course by the starboard tack yacht to avoid collision, then the starboard tack yacht would be disqualified. See Fig. 15.

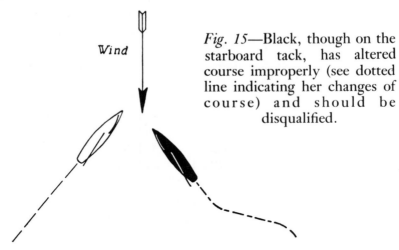

Wind

Fig. 15—Black, though on the starboard tack, has altered course improperly (see dotted line indicating her changes of course) and should be disqualified.

36.*Opposite Tacks—Basic Rule*

A *port tack* yacht shall keep clear of a *starboard tack* yacht.

This basic rule is illustrated by Figs. 16A, 16B, 16C and 16D. There are only two times when a starboard tack yacht which is not obstructing (rule 34) does not have right of way over a port tack yacht: 1. If returning from a premature start (rule 44) and 2. If overlapped by an inside port tack yacht sailing on a down wind leg of the course and about to pass or round a mark.

37.*Same Tack—Basic Rules*

37.1.*When Overlapped—A windward yacht* shall keep clear of a *leeward yacht.*

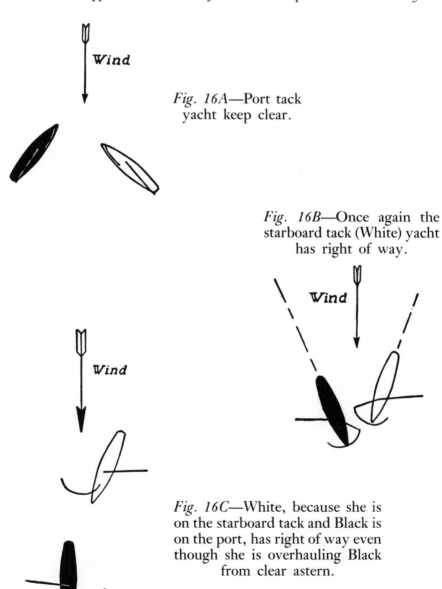

Fig. 16A—Port tack yacht keep clear.

Fig. 16B—Once again the starboard tack (White) yacht has right of way.

Fig. 16C—White, because she is on the starboard tack and Black is on the port, has right of way even though she is overhauling Black from clear astern.

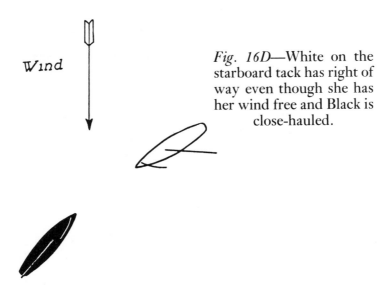

Wind

Fig. 16D—White on the starboard tack has right of way even though she has her wind free and Black is close-hauled.

37.2. *When Not Overlapped*—A yacht *clear astern* shall keep clear of a yacht *clear ahead*.

37.3. *Transitional*—A yacht which establishes an *overlap* to *leeward* from *clear astern* shall allow the *windward yacht* ample room and opportunity to keep clear.

Figures 12, 14 and 17 illustrate the basic features of this second basic rule. In each instance the white yacht has right of way. Note, however, that if clear astern a yacht must keep clear and when she establishes an overlap to leeward she must not be so close aboard that the windward yacht, in endeavoring to keep clear, strikes the leeward yacht. See Fig. 18.

38. *Same Tack—Luffing and Sailing above a Proper Course after Starting*

38.1. *Luffing Rights*—After she has *started* and cleared the starting line, a yacht *clear ahead* or a *leeward yacht* may *luff* as she pleases, subject to the *proper course* limitations of this rule.

38.2. *Proper Course Limitations*—A *leeward yacht* shall not sail above her *proper course* while an *overlap* exists, if when the *overlap* began or, at any time during its existence, the helmsman of the *windward yacht* (when sighting abeam from his normal station and sailing no higher than the *leeward yacht*) has been abreast or forward of the mainmast of the *leeward yacht*.

38.3. *Overlap Limitations*—For the purpose of this rule: An overlap does not exist unless the yachts are clearly within two overall lengths of the longer yacht; and an overlap which exists between two yachts when the leading

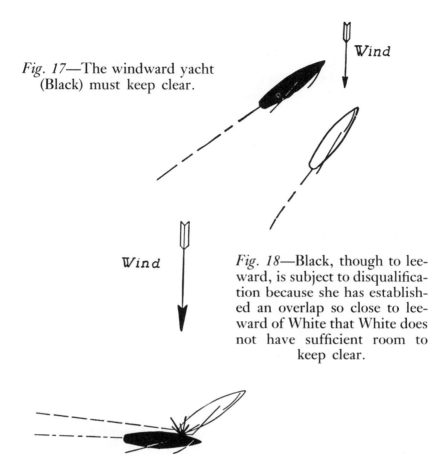

Fig. 17—The windward yacht (Black) must keep clear.

Wind

Wind

Fig. 18—Black, though to leeward, is subject to disqualification because she has established an overlap so close to leeward of White that White does not have sufficient room to keep clear.

yacht starts, or when one or both of them completes a tack or jibe, shall be regarded as a new overlap beginning at that time.

38.4.*Hailing to Stop or Prevent a Luff*—When there is doubt, the leeward yacht may assume that she has the right to luff unless the helmsman of the windward yacht has hailed "Mast Abeam," or words to that effect. The leeward yacht shall be governed by such hail, and, if she deems it improper, her only remedy is to protest.

38.5.*Curtailing a Luff*—The windward yacht shall not cause a luff to be curtailed because of her proximity to the leeward yacht unless an obstruction, a third yacht or other object restricts her ability to respond.

38.6.*Luffing Two or More Yachts*—A yacht shall not luff unless she has the right to luff all yachts which would be affected by her luff; in which case they shall all respond even if an intervening yacht or yachts would not otherwise have the right to luff.

Note that though rule 38 does not generally permit a leeward yacht to luff a windward one which was forward of "mast abeam" when the overlap began, there are actually two exceptions. If the overlap was established before the start or while the yachts were on different tacks, their relative positions at the start or upon completion of the jibe determines whether or not the leeward yacht can luff. For the sake of rule 38, the overlap is considered as starting at the completion of the jibe or at the start, whichever is applicable, and not when the yachts actually first overlapped. If the windward yacht is aft of the mast abeam position at either of these two instants, then the leeward yacht may luff. See Figs. 19 and 20.

39. *Same Tack—Sailing Below a Proper Course After Starting*

A yacht which is on a free leg of the course shall not sail below her *proper course* when she is clearly within three of her overall lengths of either a *leeward* yacht or a yacht *clear astern* which is steering a course to pass to *leeward*.

Note that this rule now applies only on leeward legs.

40. *Same Tack—Luffing Before Starting*

Before a right-of-way yacht has *started* and cleared the starting line, any *luff* on her part which causes another yacht to have to alter course to avoid a collision shall be carried out slowly and in such a way as to give a *windward* yacht room and opportunity to keep clear. However, the *leeward* yacht shall not so *luff* above a *close-hauled* course, unless the helmsman of the *windward* yacht (sighting abeam from his normal station) is abaft the mainmast of the *leeward* yacht. Rules 38.4, Hailing to Stop or Prevent a Luff; 38.5, Curtailing a Luff; and 38.6, Luffing Two or More Yachts, also apply.

By slowing down the maneuvers at the start, this rule intended to lessen fouls at a time when boats are bunched more closely than at any other time of the race. While it does not permit a sudden luff, a gradual luff is allowed.

Note particularly that the leeward yacht, before starting, may luff up to closehauled *even though* the windward yacht was forward of mast abeam. This provision was adopted in 1969 and is designed to give the leeward yacht more ammunition against boats on the line to windward of her.

41. *Changing Tacks—Tacking and Jibing*

41.1. *Basic Rule*—A yacht which is either *taching* or *jibing* shall keep clear of a yacht on a *tack*.

41.2. *Transitional*—A yacht shall neither *tack* nor *jibe* into a position which will give her right of way unless she does so far enough from a yacht *on a*

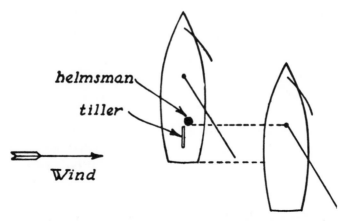

Fig. 19—Under the new rules, the leeward yacht being passed to windward, may not luff after the helmsman of the windward yacht is abeam of the leeward yacht's mast.

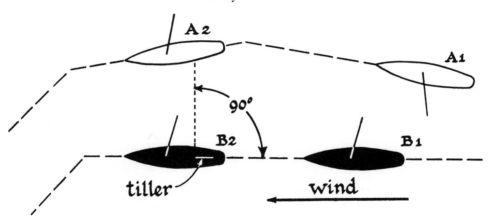

Fig. 20—A2 can luff B2 because B was not forward of A's mast line when A completed her jibe.

tack to enable this yacht to keep clear without having to begin to alter her course until after the *tack* or *jibe* has been completed.

41.3. *Onus*—A yacht which *tacks* or *jibes* has the onus of satisfying the race committee that she completed her *tack* or *jibe* in accordance with rule 41.2.

41.4. *When Simultaneous*—When two yachts are both *tacking* or both *jibing* at the same time, the one on the other's *port* side shall keep clear.

Fig. 21, which illustrates this rule, shows both yachts as gray because their rights are still to be determined. Although the yacht which has just completed her tack has right of way and the other must begin to keep clear at this stage, if the latter does begin and still strikes the starboard tack yacht, the former is disqualified for having tacked too close. A similar condition exists in the case of a yacht which has just jibed onto the starboard tack in close proximity to a port tack yacht.

Note in particular that the port tack yacht does not have to *begin* to alter course to keep clear until the other yacht has completed her tack or jibe onto starboard tack. This provision and also the onus of proof prevents tacking or jibing too close. "Onus of proving," however, should be interpreted as onus of satisfying the race committee that the rule was not infringed, since absolute proof is almost impossible. If "proof" were interpreted literally it would result in throwing out the tacking yacht whenever the other claimed the tack was too close. The committee must be satisfied that the tack was not made too close but need not have absolute proof.

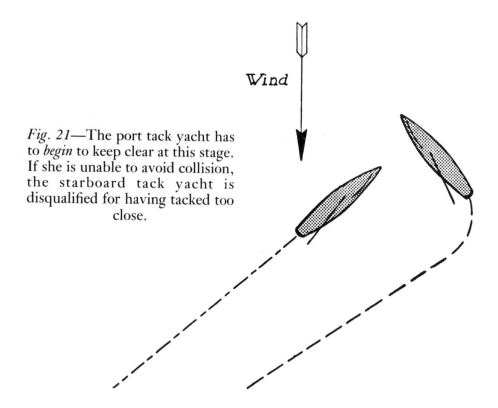

Wind

Fig. 21—The port tack yacht has to *begin* to keep clear at this stage. If she is unable to avoid collision, the starboard tack yacht is disqualified for having tacked too close.

SECTION C—RULES WHICH APPLY AT MARKS AND OBSTRUCTIONS AND OTHER EXCEPTIONS TO THE RULES OF SECTION B

When a rule of this section applies, to the extent to which it explicitly provides rights and obligations, it over-rides any conflicting rule of Section B, Principal Right of Way Rules and their Limitations, except rule 35 (Limitations on Altering Course).

42. *Rounding or Passing Marks and Obstructions*

42.1. *Room at Marks and Obstructions When Overlapped*—When yachts are about to round or pass a *mark*, other than a starting *mark* surrounded by navigable water, on the same required side or an *obstruction* on the same side:

(a)   An outside yacht shall give each yacht *overlapping* her on the inside, room to round or pass the *mark* or *obstruction*, except as provided in rules 42.1(c), 42.1(d) and 42.4 (At a Starting Mark Surrounded by Navigable Water).

Room includes room for an *overlapping* yacht to *tack* or *jibe* when either is an integral part of the rounding or passing manoeuvre.

(b)   When an inside yacht of two or more *overlapped* yachts either on opposite *tacks*, or on the same *tack* without *luffing* rights, will have to *jibe* in order most directly to assume a *proper course* to the next *mark*, she shall *jibe* at the first reasonable opportunity.

(c)   When two yachts on opposite *tacks* are on a beat or when one of them will have to *tack* either to round the *mark* or to avoid the *obstruction*, as between each other, rule 42.1 shall not apply and they are subject to rules 36, Opposite Tacks—Basic Rule, and 41, Changing Tacks—Tacking and Jibing.

(d)   An outside *leeward yacht* with luffing rights may take an inside yacht to windward of a *mark* provided that she hails to that effect and begins to *luff* before she is within two of her overall lengths of the *mark* and provided that she also passes to windward of it.

42.2. *Clear Astern and Clear Ahead in the Vicinity of Marks and Obstructions*— When yachts are about to round or pass a *mark*, other than a starting *mark* surrounded by navigable water, on the same required side or an *obstruction* on the same side:

(a)   A yacht *clear astern* shall keep clear in anticipation of and during the rounding or passing manoeuvre when the yacht *clear ahead* remains on the same *tack* or *jibes*.

(b)   A yacht *clear ahead* which *tacks to round a mark* is subject to rule 41 (Changing Tacks—Tacking and Jibing), but a yacht *clear astern* shall not *luff* above *close-hauled* so as to prevent the yacht *clear ahead* from *tacking*.

42.3. *Limitations on Establishing and Maintaining an Overlap in the Vicinity of Marks and Obstructions*

(a)   When a yacht *clear astern* establishes an inside *overlap* she shall be
      entitled to room under rule 42.1(a) (Room at Marks and Obstruc-
      tions when Overlapped) only when the yacht *clear ahead:*
      (i)   is able to give the required room and
      (ii)   is outside two of her overall lengths of the *mark* or *obstruction*,
             except when one of the yachts has completed a *tack* within two
             overall lengths of the *mark* or *obstruction*, or when the *obstruc-
             tion* is a continuing one as provided in rule 42.3(f).

(b)   A yacht *clear ahead* shall be under no obligation to give room to a
      yacht *clear astern* before an *overlap* is established.

(c)   When an outside yacht is *overlapped* at the time she comes within
      two of her overall lengths of a *mark* or an *obstruction*, she shall
      continue to be bound by rule 42.1(a) (Room at Marks and Obstruc-
      tions when Overlapped) to give room as required even though the
      overlap is thereafter broken.

(d)   A yacht which claims an inside *overlap* has the onus of satisfying the
      race committee that the overlap was established in proper time.

(e)   An outside yacht which claims to have broken an *overlap* has the
      onus of satisfying the race committee that she became *clear ahead*
      when she was more than two of her overall lengths from the *mark or
      obstruction*.

(f)   A yacht *clear astern* may establish an *overlap* between the yacht *clear
      ahead* and a continuing *obstruction* such as a shoal or the shore or
      another vessel, only when at that time there is room for her to pass
      between them in safety.

42.4. *At a Starting Mark Surrounded by Navigable Water*

When approaching the starting line to *start*, a *leeward yacht* shall be
under no obligation to give any *windward yacht* room to pass to leeward
of a starting *mark* surrounded by navigable water; but, after the starting
signal, a *leeward yacht* shall not deprive a *windward yacht* of room at such a
mark by sailing either above the compass bearing of the course to the first
mark or above *close-hauled*.

Figs. 22A, 22B and 22C show when an overlap can and cannot be claimed.
Note particularly that it cannot be claimed after the leading yacht is within 2
lengths of the mark except when tacking at a windward mark as permitted by
rule 42.2(b).

As stated earlier, 42.1 presents one of the two times when a starboard tack
yacht has to keep clear of a port tack one, namely when the port tack yacht has
an inside overlap at a leeward mark.

42.4 is one of the most significant of all the new rules. It is intended to
eliminate barging (reaching off for the line and forcing room at the windward

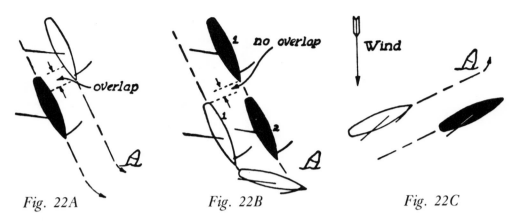

Fig. 22A   Fig. 22B   Fig. 22C

Fig. 22A—White has an overlap and can claim room.

Fig. 22B—Forcing an overlap *after* the leading boat is
within 2 lengths of the mark is illegal.

Fig. 22C—The trailing boat has no overlap but has right of way because
the leader cannot complete her tack without fouling the trailing boat.

end) and it actually does. Under the rules in effect right after World War II, a
leeward yacht had to, after the starting gun had fired, give room between
herself and the windward starting marker to all yachts that had an overlap.
Under this new rule she need give no such room but may not sail above close-
hauled, if the first leg is to windward, or above the course to the first mark, if
the first leg is a leeward one, in order to deprive a windward yacht of room. In
Fig. 23, yachts A, B, and C need not give room to E, F, and D.

43. *Close-Hauled, Hailing for Room to Tack at Obstructions*

43.1. *Hailing*—When two *close-hauled* yachts are on the same *tack* and safe
pilotage requires the yacht *clear ahead* or the *leeward yacht* to make a
substantial alteration of course to clear an *obstruction*, and when she
intends to *tack*, but cannot *tack* without colliding with the other yacht,
she shall hail the other yacht for room to *tack* and clear the other yacht,
but she shall not hail and *tack* simultaneously.

43.2. *Responding*—The hailed yacht at the earliest possible moment after the
hail shall either:
(a)   *tack*, in which case, the hailing yacht shall begin to *tack* either:
       (i)   before the hailed yacht has completed her *tack*, or
       (ii)   if she cannot then *tack* without colliding with the hailed yacht,
              immediately she is able to *tack* and clear her, or

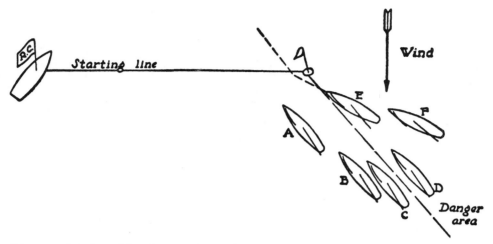

Fig. 23—Under old rules, A, B, and C had to give room to E, F, and D *after* the starting gun had fired. Under the new rules, they need not give room. D and F will therefore be forced out, and must either kill way or tack. E is lucky and just has room to cross to windward of A and ahead of C without fouling either. After the gun fires, A and B must not sail above close-hauled and therefore C, under the new rules, just has room to pass between B and the mark.

      (*b*)   reply "You *tack*," or words to that effect, when in her opinion she can keep clear without *tacking* or after postponing her *tack*. In this case:
           (i)   the hailing yacht shall immediately *tack* and
           (ii)   the hailed yacht shall keep clear.
           (iii) The onus of satisfying the race committee that she kept clear shall lie on the hailed yacht which replied "You *tack*."

43.3.*Limitation on Right to Room to Tack When the Obstruction Is also a Mark*
      (*a*)   When the hailed yacht can fetch an *obstruction* which is also a *mark*, the hailing yacht shall not be entitled to room to *tack* and clear the hailed yacht and the hailed yacht shall immediately so inform the hailing yacht.
      (*b*)   If, thereafter, the hailing yacht again hails for room to tack and clear the hailed yacht, the hailed yacht shall, at the earliest possible moment after the hail, give the hailing yacht the required room. After receiving room, the hailing yacht shall either retire immediately or exonerate herself by accepting an alternative penalty when so prescribed in the sailing instructions.
      (*c*)   When, after having refused to respond to a hail under rule 43.3(a), the hailed yacht fails to fetch, she shall retire immediately, or exonerate herself by accepting an alternative penalty when so prescribed in the sailing instructions.

Note that when the windward yacht is required to give the leeward yacht room to tack, she can do so either by tacking or by killing way. In either event, as soon as such room is given, the leeward yacht must tack at once. See Fig. 24A.

Fig. 24B illustrates the cases in which the windward yacht need not give room at an obstruction which she can clear without tacking, since the obstruction is a mark.

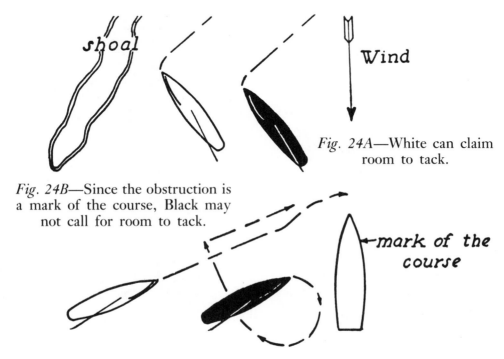

shoal

Wind

Fig. 24A—White can claim room to tack.

Fig. 24B—Since the obstruction is a mark of the course, Black may not call for room to tack.

mark of the course

44.*Returning to Start*

44.1.(*a*)   After the starting signal is made, a premature starter returning to *start*, or a yacht working into position from the course side of the starting line or its extensions, shall keep clear of all yachts which are *starting*, or have *started*, correctly, until she is wholly on the pre-start side of the starting line or its extensions.

    (*b*)   Thereafter, she shall be accorded the rights under the rules of Part IV of a yacht which is *starting* correctly; but when she thereby acquires right of way over another yacht which is *starting* correctly, she shall allow that yacht ample room and opportunity to keep clear.

44.2.A premature starter while continuing to sail the course and until it is obvious that she is returning to *start*, shall be accorded the rights under the rules of Part IV of a yacht which has *started*.

As noted earlier, this is one of the two times that a starboard tack yacht does not have right of way over a port tack yacht. It should be emphasized, however, that even though early at the start, until she is returning she does retain her normal right of way.

45.*Re-rounding after Touching a Mark*

45.1.A yacht which has touched a *mark* and is exonerating herself in accordance with rule 52.2, Touching a Mark, shall keep clear of all other yachts which are about to round or pass it or have rounded or passed it correctly, until she has rounded it completely and has cleared it and is on a *proper course* to the next *mark*.

45.2.A yacht which has touched a *mark* while continuing to sail the course and until it is obvious that she is returning to round it completely in accordance with rule 52.2, Touching a Mark, shall be accorded rights under the rules of Part IV.

This rule was brand new in 1969. Previously one had to drop out of the race after touching a mark. Rule 52.2 referred to in this rule now allows re-rounding instead.

46.*Anchored, Aground, Capsized or Person Overboard*

46.1.A yacht under way shall keep clear of another yacht *racing* which is anchored, aground, capsized, or rescuing a person overboard. Of two anchored yachts, the one which anchored later shall keep clear, except that a yacht which is dragging shall keep clear of one which is not.

46.2.A yacht anchored or aground shall indicate the fact to any yacht which may be in danger of fouling her. Unless the size of the yachts or the weather conditions make some other signal necessary, a hail is sufficient indication.

46.3.A yacht shall not be penalized for fouling a yacht in distress which she is attempting to assist nor a yacht which goes aground or capsizes immediately ahead of her.

That brings us to the end of the right of way rules, rules which, if thoroughly, almost instinctively, understood, can let the skipper concentrate on the many other aspects of winning a race.

IV

Training the Crew

RACING A BOAT is fun. If it were not, thousands of persons wouldn't be spending all summer doing it and much of the winter looking forward to next year. Although the title of this chapter may sound a bit business-like for a sport which is followed for pleasure, a bit of training actually adds to the enjoyment. Most people prefer to do well rather than poorly in a race. Training helps achieve that end and in addition, a crew which works smoothly together has more fun, greater relaxation and less fuss in the course of a race.

By training we really mean practice. It can be done whenever the entire crew is out for a sail or heading to or from a race and feels in the mood. The very best sailors do it. Why shouldn't you?

Assign Specific Jobs

The first step in training is for the skipper to assign each crew member a job. Say the crew totals four, including the skipper. One man might be assigned the leeward jib sheet when on the wind, the spinnaker sheet when it is set and the jib halliard. Another might handle backstays (if any), the weather jib sheet, the spinnaker halliard and spinnaker guys. A third might be directed to take care of the main sheet while beating to windward, and the forward deck station for handling light sails when setting, dousing or jibing is in progress. The skipper has a lot to keep him busy at the tiller and thinking of tactics, watching for slants, etc., but he might be able to lend a hand on the main sheet during some maneuvers.

Other jobs should be detailed regularly. When starting, some skippers prefer to keep their own time and others like to have one of the crew record it and call it out at intervals. It is well to have one of the more experienced crew members help the skipper look for and report wind shifts, stronger breezes and the progress of competitors. The point is, no matter how large or small the crew, each member should have a definite job at all times and during all

45

maneuvers throughout the race. Results are never as smooth if duties are assigned haphazardly. It may be more fun if positions are rotated among the crew from week to week. This gives each a better idea of the overall problem and results eventually in greater efficiency. But it is well to keep assignments unchanged during the course of any one race.

Keep Crew Weight Evenly Distributed

Not only should jobs be detailed but it is advisable also to tell each man where he should keep his weight. We have already noticed the importance of keeping the boat trimmed to her lines. All the crew should be so stationed as to maintain this trim and at the same time be able to work the ship effectively. As one man goes forward to handle the headsails, his weight should be compensated for by another going aft. At all other times, the weight of the crew should be concentrated as close to the middle (in fore and aft direction) of the boat as is practicable. It is important to prevent their weight being spread out unnecessarily. If it is, the boat's ends are made heavier, she is apt to hobbyhorse and is slowed down slightly.

As skipper, you should explain to the crew that you want more weight to leeward in light going than in a breeze. Let them know how strong the wind must be before you want them to lie or hike out to windward. In a variable wind, the crew should be shifting their weight to leeward or to windward as the wind dictates and without any word from the skipper. It is in just such a breeze that he is busiest with other problems.

Once assignments have been made, training boils down to going through the more common evolutions. In all such practice, make it as realistic as possible.

Practice Starts

Some time when you are out sailing, locate a pair of moorings or government buoys which simulate a starting line. Start a stopwatch and announce to all hands that you are going to go through the motions of starting, that the start will be in exactly ten minutes, that the boat will be crossing the line on such and such a course and that the spinnaker will be desired. Then jockey around in the vicinity of the line. While the skipper is timing his approaches the crew is busy working the ship and getting the spinnaker ready under conditions similar to those which will be met on race day. Finally the time is up, the skipper sees how close he came to hitting the line "on the gun" with full way on and the crew has the practice of setting the spinnaker smartly and at the correct instant.

For emergency training it might be well if the skipper got over too early on purpose (with spinnaker up) and then see how fast the boat could be brought back to recross the line.

Practice Sail Handling Around Marks

Similar practice in rounding marks will save many seconds and much shouting when race day rolls around. Approach a buoy with spinnaker set, give the order to douse spinnaker, hoist jib and then actually round the mark when you reach it. Not only will the crew learn to work smoothly and quickly under the press of limited time, but you will get a definite idea of how much time is required to complete the sail handling and to have everything in order when the mark is reached. This knowledge permits carrying the light sails as long as practicable in a race, thus saving valuable seconds, and prevents carrying them too long with the possible loss of minutes should they become jammed aloft, or dragged overboard because of trying to carry them too long.

Rehearse jibing around marks, sometimes with spinnaker being jibed in the process and at other times either dousing it or setting it on the new course. In short, practice all the various approaches which might occur in a race and get in as many different types of sail drill as are likely to be encountered. Work not so much for speed as for smoothness and to avoid getting and sails fouled up. Speed will then follow. A well-trained crew is able to jibe the modern parachute spinnakers without having the sail break more than momentarily, if at all.

Practice Tacking

In your training don't overlook the simple act of tacking. A boat comes about so frequently in the course of a race that if one yard of advance can be gained on each tack a winning margin might soon be built up. Train the crew to realize that when you say "ready about" they take their stations quietly, remove excess turns from the cleats but change the trim not at all. At the command "hard-a-lee" the helm is put down; leeward jib sheet is let fly seconds later (but not until after a break in the luff) and leeward runners start coming home. Make sure that the man on the weather jib sheet (the leeward sheet on the new tack) doesn't trim too soon. Up until the boat is head to wind, he only takes in slack. From then on, he trims fast with at least two turns on the winch so that what he gains won't be lost when strain occurs as the jib fills. Then he winches the jib in quickly to the desired trim. It is impossible to overemphasize the importance of not trimming too soon. Doing so will tend to back the jib and is sure to slow the boat down. If one trims too late it is hard to get the jib flat enough, especially in a strong breeze. Again, practice makes perfect.

And the Skipper Learns About Wind

While out on these practice sails, the skipper should increase his knowledge of wind. Wind is his boat's motor and when the race comes he will want to know how to get the most out of the "motor." It is most important that he learn to detect the direction of the wind and changes in its strength and direction. This he can feel on his face, can see on the sails, on the water, and can detect through telltales, wind pennants, cigarette smoke, or shore based smoke. He can learn the way the wind hauls off the shore, funnels into bays and, through repeated observation, will learn much about the local vagaries of the wind. We will touch on all of this in greater detail in subsequent chapters, but it seems not too early to urge beginners (readers who are experienced sailors need no urging) to become wind conscious and to get to know it well.

There is no need to labor the point further that practice beforehand can save lots of time when the race begins. Many crews never take the little time that is required, yet it is hard to realize why not. Anyone who has tried practicing will aver that it is fun and that it adds variety to a leisurely sail, providing it isn't continued for too long at a time. Above all, it helps win races.

V

The Day of the Race

WE HAVE BOUGHT our boat, tuned her, learned the racing rules and even trained our crew. The day of a race is at hand. Surely we must be ready to go. Well, not completely. There is still lots to be done before the start. Fortunately, most racing men find it all an enjoyable part of the sport.

Box or Stop Light Sails at Home

Even before leaving home it is advisable to trace or stop the spinnaker and other light sails (if any). Before doing so, examine the sail to detect tears or snags from a previous race which could enlarge into serious tears if neglected.

For mending small holes there are several makes of sail repair tape, available from most sailmakers or from marine supply stores. They work wonderfully well.

Just thirty years ago most skippers owning boats 20 feet or more stopped their spinnakers. Today only large boat owners should and then only in a strong breeze. Even on large ocean racers it is now common to set the spinnaker flying from a bag. This method will be described in detail in Chapter IX but for those who do own truly large yachts and who prefer to stop sails on small boats in strong winds it might prove helpful to review the proper method of stopping.

When ready to begin stopping, a neater job can be done if the sail is stretched out on a dry lawn; there is always danger of getting it wet if stopped on board. For stopping twine, light worsted or yarn is recommended, since it is easiest to work with and may be unravelled to a single strand for stopping the upper part of the sail where less strength is required.

After the sail has been stretched out, fasten the head and the tacks so that the luff and leech are in tension during the whole stopping operation. If the skirt of the sail is long, as in some parachute spinnakers, fold it up into the middle. Next, starting at the top, bunch or roll the sail, being sure to keep

49

both leech and luff exposed and not rolled up in the sail. I prefer rolling rather than bunching the sail, providing the leech and luff are not rolled in. A rolled sail is neater, easier to handle, stow, and hoist, not so apt to foul cotter pins or other projections and less prone to break out prematurely. If done properly, it breaks out just as easily as a bunched spinnaker. Commence tieing stops at the head of the sail and work down. Don't place a stop nearer than two feet to the head, because it might then be difficult to break. Tie other stops close together, as close as a foot and a half and, as you near the foot, a second turn is desirable. This will prevent premature breaking and will permit hoisting the sail well in advance of the time it will be broken out. At the very foot you may want three turns of stopping yarn as an added precaution. And when you are through, remember to take the stopping yarn on board in case the sail is set more than once in the course of the race. If the wind is light, every other stop can be broken out before hoisting.

After the sail is stopped, fold it back and forth in a bundle about three feet long, with the head on one end and the tacks on the other, and tie a couple of turns of heavy stopping yarn around each end. Then the whole sail can be carried on board knowing it is in perfect condition for hoisting, with no turns in it. The final two stops are broken just before hoisting.

Check Weather Reports

Just before leaving home it is advisable to check the latest weather, either through reports on the radio or by calling the Weather Bureau. This gives a tentative guide on the sail you will want to use and sometimes gives an indication of impending wind shifts which may occur during the race. For example, if a light and variable easterly prevails at your locality and a weather station reports fresh southerly winds 20 to 50 miles to the south, there is good reason to expect them to reach your locality before or during the race.

Read the Circular at Home

I have found it helpful to read the race circular at home. Once, after failing to do so, I learned later that I was mistaken as to the location of that day's race and, consequently, almost missed the start. Become acquainted with possible courses and give some thought to the way each should be sailed under the expected conditions. Check the time the tide turns and decide beforehand what effect it will have on the race and how it can be combatted or utilized most effectively. Study current charts at home also. Check, of course, your starting time and read the entire circular through till you have the various facts well in hand. It is difficult to do all this on board, especially after you are under way.

A typical race circular is reproduced in this chapter. Others may differ in details but all are easy to understand after a bit of study. This circular, like those printed by the more active yacht clubs, is clear and needs no explanation. If beginners study it, they should find nothing confusing in their own club's circular when they come to use it.

It is a good idea to place the circular between two sheets of clear plastic and bind the outside with adhesive tape. The circular will not get wet, and is easy to read in the wind since the plastic stiffens it. New or different circulars are inserted easily by stripping the tape off two sides and sealing up again.

Don't Forget Equipment

Before dashing out of the house, take a moment to check if you have everything you need (a check list isn't a bad idea)—stopwatch, sails, binoculars, bailer, etc. We once forgot our spinnaker; there were two leeward legs that day and no celebration at home that night.

Get to the Boat Early

No amount of preparation at home is as important as getting to the boat early. Don't rush aboard at the last minute and set off half-cocked. There is too much to be done, none of which takes much time but all of which should be done carefully and without fail. First pump the boat out and then sponge the last drop of water from her. Look under all the floor boards and insure that none of the limber holes is clogged and that no water is trapped.

Next, if any sails were left on board, make sure they are entirely dry and, if not, hoist them or spread them out. Check running rigging to insure that none needs replacing. Add a few drops of oil to the working part of winches and blocks, if they are at all stiff. Make sure that cotter pins or other sharp projections are carefully taped over. If you like to sail with ribbon telltales on the shrouds and backstays, untangle these and replace as necessary. All gear that is not apt to be used in the race should be stowed neatly and *as low as possible*. Remember, the rules forbid *shifting* the boat's equipment during the race so that it may not serve as movable ballast, but they do not prevent putting this equipment in the most desirable place. Not only locate the gear low (even under the floor boards if it is not easily damaged and will fit) but also make sure that it is so placed that proper fore and aft trim will not be impaired.

NOROTON YACHT CLUB

RACE INSTRUCTIONS......

RULES - Racing rules of the N.A.Y.R.U. shall govern racing procedure and decisions. In addition all Yachts must conform to the rules of their respective classes.

NOTICES - Official notices and Starting Times will be posted on the Bulletin Board on the Club Terrace, and it is the responsibility of each Crew to check this Board for information.

Notices when posted by the Race Committee on the Board shall be deemed to have been delivered to each Crew, provided, however, that such instructions may be superceded by verbal instructions by the Race Committee, duly given by it to the Helmsman of each Crew prior to the making of the Warning signal.

COURSES - Courses will be windward-leeward, or triangular and may then have an extra leg. Races may also be started in the middle of the windward leg. Triangular courses may or may not be equilateral. All marks of the course are to be passed on the same side as the starting mark. Note method of signalling courses below.

GOVERNMENT MARKS - All Government Marks may be disregarded with the exception of Smith's Reef Red Nun Bouy number 30 which must be passed on channel side except when used as a mark of the course.

PROTESTS - Protest Flag must be flown from the time of foul until after crossing finish line. All reasonable effort should be made to notify competitor at time of the foul of intention to protest. Protest must be in writing and be in the hands of the Protest Committee within twenty-four hours after the Committee Boat returns. Skippers, Crews and Witnesses must report to the Protest Committee within 48 hours after Committee Boat returns. Time requirements for Protest in Special events may be modified.

STARTING SIGNALS FOR FIRST CLASS - Each cylinder shall remain hoisted for 4 and 1/2 minutes.

    1. WARNING SIGNAL: 10 minutes before Start hoisting of WHITE cylinder. GUN.

    2. PREPARATORY SIGNAL: 5 minutes before Start hoisting of BLUE cylinder. GUN.

    3. START: Hoisting of RED cylinder. GUN.

MISFIRE - The Hoisting of the cylinder indicates the signal if the gun is misfired.

STARTING AND FINISHING LINE - The line will be between the starting mark and a WHITE flag on the Committee Boat. RED cylinder indicates Committee Boat is on station at the finish line.

RECALL - A WHITE cylinder with RED horizontal band accompanied by a short blast of a horn for each Yacht recalled. The sail number of recalled Yachts will be announced verbally from Committee Boat. However, failure to hear his number does not relieve the Skipper of his responsibility to make a proper start.

GENERAL RECALL FOR CLASS STARTING - TWO GUNS and hoisting of Recall cylinder. The Recall cylinder will remain hoisted for 4 and 1/2 minutes timed from the first of the Two Guns mentioned in the previous sentence. Upon lowering of Recall cylinder the PREPARATORY signal for the Class recalled will be made 30 seconds later.

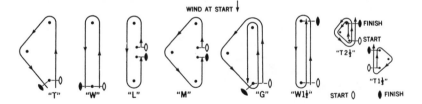

WIND AT START

"T" "W" "L" "M" "G" "W1½" START () "T2½" "T1½" FINISH START ● FINISH

COURSE SIGNALS.....

1. The diagrams above indicate the kind of courses that may be used. The letter correspond-ing to the course to be sailed will be displayed on the Committee Boat prior to the Warning Gun. Only Noroton Special Markers will be used with the courses signalled by "T", "W", "L", "M", and "G". Nun number 28, designated on the chart as "N" is to be considered a Noroton Special Marker when these signals are used. Number indicates laps, complete or partial.

"T" - Triangle.
"W" - Windward and leeward.
"L" - Windward, leeward, windward.
"M" - Triangle with start and finish in middle of leg.
"G" - Modified Gold Cup Course.

Distance of each leg approximately 1 and 1/4 miles for triangular courses and approximately 1 and 1/2 miles for windward - leeward.

2. Government Marks may be used as Racing Marks in special situations and their letters will be signalled in the order of rounding. In such case, disregard paragraph 1 above. A Noroton Special Marker may be set as the windward mark and signalled by Committee Boat displaying this card: [▶] Number indicates laps, complete or partial.

Panels with Black letters on Yellow field indicate diagramed courses.

Panels with Yellow letters on Black field indicate number of laps, complete or partial.

Panels with Black letters on White field indicate courses using Government Marks.

SPECIAL NOTE: When the following signals are given a panel simulating Code Flag may be used. However, a Code Flag will be used for the purpose of timing the signal and the panel displayed later at the convenience of the Race Committee.

POSTPONEMENT - Code Flag "P" (BLUE with WHITE square); TWO GUNS. All races not started, postponed until later in the day. Upon lowering "P"; ONE GUN. Either Warning sign-al or "O" will be made 30 seconds after lowering of "P".

NO RACE OR CANCELLATION - Code Flag "N" (BLUE and WHITE CHECKERED); TWO GUNS. All races, including those in progress cancelled until later in the day. Upon lowering "N" ONE GUN. Either Warning signal or "O" will replace "N" 30 seconds after lowering.

RACE OFF - Code Flag "O" (YELLOW and RED triangles) THREE GUNS. All races including those in progress are off for the day.

SHORTENING OF COURSE - Code Flag "S" (WHITE with BLUE square) TWO GUNS. Finish between WHITE Flag on Committee Boat and Mark. RED cylinder indicates that Committee Boat is on station at the finish line.

MARK MISSING - Code Flag "M" (WHITE diagonal cross on BLUE field); "Mark has shifted and this vessel is the Mark."

COME WITHIN HAIL - Hoisting of Code Flag "Q" (YELLOW square).

TIME LIMIT - A time limit of three hours will apply, unless otherwise specified. Local class rules apply.

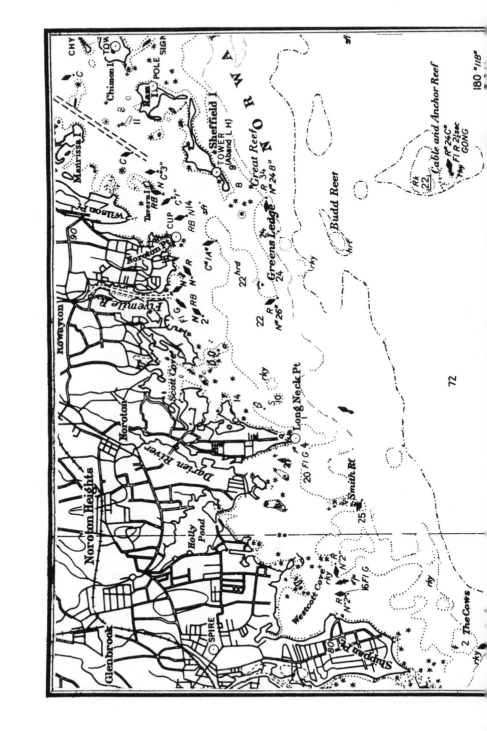

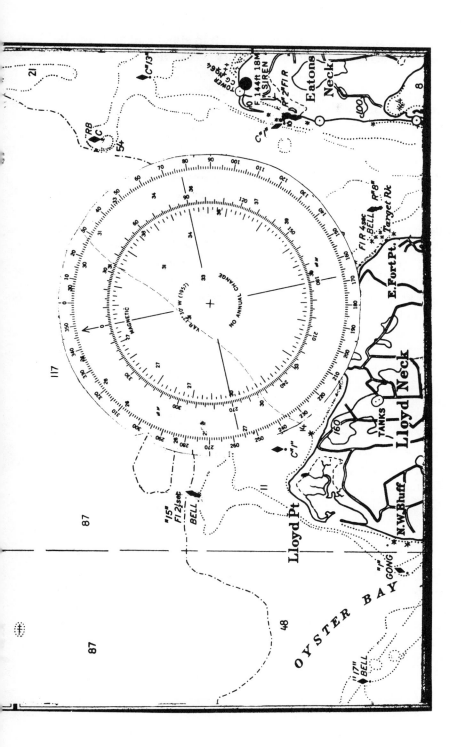

Don't forget to rub down the bottom and topsides in the manner previously outlined. They can be made clean and smooth in about half an hour. Be sure to allow this time before the first race of every week-end.

The sails should be bent last of all. Being left in the bag until then, they remain dry while pumping and other work is going on. And the longer one waits, the better the chances of bending the sail best suited to the wind which will prevail after the race starts. If it is a long distance to the starting line, leave the mooring with an old sail set and change it to the racing suit upon arrival. Every sail has just so many hours of racing built into it and its efficient life can be lengthened by using it only in a race. In rainy weather, it is doubly important to bend the racing sails as short a time before the start as practicable. Doing so enables them to keep lighter and to retain their shape. Dacron sails are affected less adversely by rain than the cotton sails we used to sail with but, even so, it makes sense to keep them dry as long as possible.

Except in small boats don't worry about the added weight of an extra sail. If it is stowed in the right fore and aft position and as low as possible, at worst it will be of little harm and it may be very useful. In a breeze, the added weight is actually helpful to boats of certain types.

Arrive at the Start Before the First Gun

In any event, leave the mooring soon enough to arrive at the line early, preferably before the warning gun for the first class. This gives an opportunity to run the line when it is clear of starters and to make a tentative decision as to which is the more favorable end. It is fun before the race to sail amid the gathering fleet, waving to competitors or friends in other classes who can be seen only at this stage.

Starting the Watch

No matter how late your start may be, start with your watch on one of the first guns. This permits checking it later on to see that it is keeping time. Be sure to start and check the watch upon seeing the puff of smoke from the gun, rather than waiting for the report. It takes five seconds for sound to travel one mile and even one or two seconds may mean the difference between getting your wind clear or being covered at the start. If a horn is being used instead of a gun, look for the hoisting of the visual signal and check the watch by it.

Watch Other Classes Start

If other classes are starting before yours, watch their starts carefully. By so doing, much can be learned about the most favorable end of the line. If time permits, it is worth while following the earlier classes for a short distance, at least by eye. You may find some indication of which boats are faring best and thereby get a lead on the course to follow. Conditions may change by the time you are starting but at least you will have gained an indication of what to expect.

Check Course Signals

As soon as course signals for your class have been hoisted, check them in the circular. Do it carefully and have another person confirm your interpretation. Write the signals down. Almost every year, races are lost because of a too hurried reading of the circular.

Ten Minutes to Go

The gun ten minutes before your start is the warning. In the next five minutes the class ahead of yours will be jockeying for the start. It is necessary to keep out of the restricted area to give them a free hand but it is prudent to keep as near to the line as you can without causing interference. Once they have crossed, the restricted area will be yours and you will want to be in it every second of the five minute interval to plan your start. All your preparation of the days and hours before this time will be of real value and it is a satisfying feeling to realize that you, your boat and your crew are "right." But the following five minutes and your position as the starting gun goes off are in themselves of such importance that they merit a chapter of their own.

VI

Starting Tactics

A BOAT'S POSITION at the start is the greatest single determining factor in the average yacht race. Some sailors who really know their stuff say that in a well-matched one-design class, the position at the start is half the race. In an open class, where the boats are of many designs, a fast one often comes from behind, finally to capture the lead and go on to win, but this happens far less often in a well matched fleet. In the latter instance, the two or three boats that get the jump usually stay out in front especially in a steady wind. Everything works in their favor—a clear wind, smooth sea, and the ability to go just where they want to. The slow starters either have to take a bitter dose of backwind and a broken sea or "take a flyer" and sail a risky course to clear their wind, with the usually vain hope for a break which will enable them to sail around boats that they can't sail through.

Since the ability to start well is such a tremendous asset, the five minutes after the preparatory gun merit special consideration. It is in this interval that the groundwork of the start is made. The skipper has already made a tentative decision about which end of the line to cross and what course he expects to follow. Now he must commit himself to a final decision. There is no time to lose.

Which End to Cross?

In deciding which end of the line to cross, one must be long sighted. The average skipper is apt to underrate the importance of this decision. "Obviously," he concludes, "the end which is nearer the first mark is the better." But this is only part of the story and the good starter never overlooks any consideration. For example, one end may be the shorter by a couple of lengths. The chances are, therefore, that the bulk of the fleet will choose that end, but only one of them will get the start and have a clear wind. Now, provided your boat is faster than the average, might it not be better to take the other end, which is only a couple of lengths behind, and thereby avoid crowding? By so doing, you will be more apt to get a clear wind and sea and, if your boat is fast, you can overcome the original disadvantage. If you have the knack of usually leading the fleet across the line, then by all means play for the better end, but the mediocre starter with a fast boat would do well to consider the other.

Starting Off Wind

When an off the wind start is being made, the end which will eventually give the inside berth at the first mark, though it might appear less favorable at first, is often the better one, especially in large fleets. Furthermore, the lee-

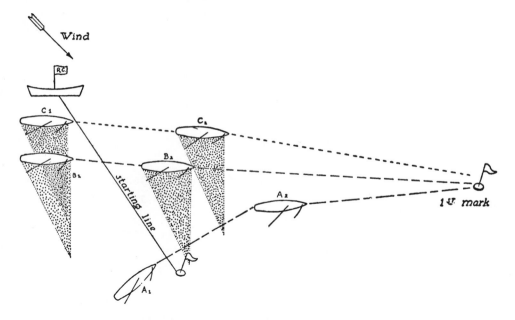

Fig. 25—Boat A, by getting a good leeward start, keeps her wind clear and, by reaching up, gains on the windward boat. B is blanketed by C and drops astern.

ward end in light air is frequently advantageous inasmuch as it enables the boat to reach up and gain greater speed from the sharper angle. A start at the leeward end, though, is always risky; it must be a good one if you are to avoid being blanketed by the boats to windward. (Fig. 25).

A Windward Start

It is even more important to get a good start when the first leg is to windward. In this case, a skipper should plan the course he will sail later before selecting the end to cross. Of course, starboard tack should always be used unless the line is a very poor one. Suppose, however, that the leeward end is favored slightly but that the skipper wishes to go on the port tack soon after the start in order to sail into a favoring slant over to the right? Would it not be better, then, to take the weather end even though a few lengths astern, so that you will be sure to be able to swing on to the port tack whenever you wish? A skipper down to leeward in the number one spot might be held against his will on the starboard tack until far enough ahead to clear the bows of those behind him on the weather quarter. By this time, some boat up to windward may have already gone on to the port tack, sailed into the good slant, and have overcome tenfold the tiny initial disadvantage and taken the lead. The clever starter always looks ahead and the man who is leading a few minutes after the gun is the one who really got the start. (Figs. 26, A, B and C).

Timing the Approach

Once the skipper has decided which end to cross, he should begin to time his approach. As soon as the restricted area is clear of a class that may be starting earlier, he should begin running the line, sailing all around the chosen end and timing the number of seconds it requires to cover all distances and make all maneuvers. One good starter of our acquaintance seldom approached the right end of the line until just before the gun, hoping, we imagine, that by hovering at the other end he might lure some unfortunates into concluding that that was the favorable end of the line, thus giving him a clearer opening at the proper end. This strategy worked for a while but soon few of the class were fooled. It seems likely now that our good starter would be even better if he used more time for practice and less for strategy but this case illustrated one of the number of tricks and tactics which may be used in making a good start.

It is advisable for the skipper to decide upon the exact course he will sail when approaching the line, and then make as many trial runs over it as time will permit. It must be remembered that during the actual start the fleet, cutting the wind and kicking up a sea, will slow the boat down, so that one should always allow more time to cover the same distance and make the same maneuvers than when practicing.

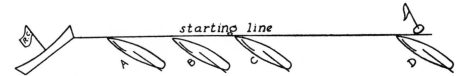

Fig. 26A—Boat A is leading at the start but B and C keep her from tacking. D is behind but is able to tack at once.

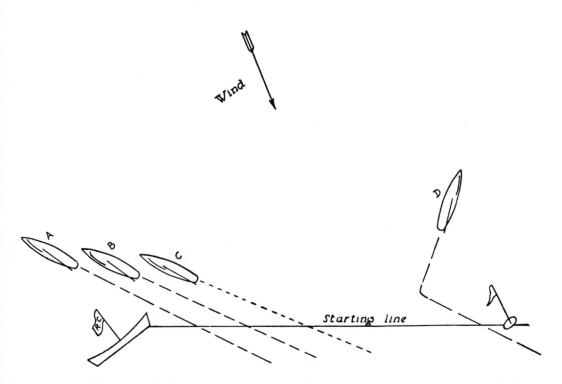

Fig. 26B—D tacks to get into a favoring slant. A, still in the lead, backwinds B and C and gains on them but is still unable to tack.

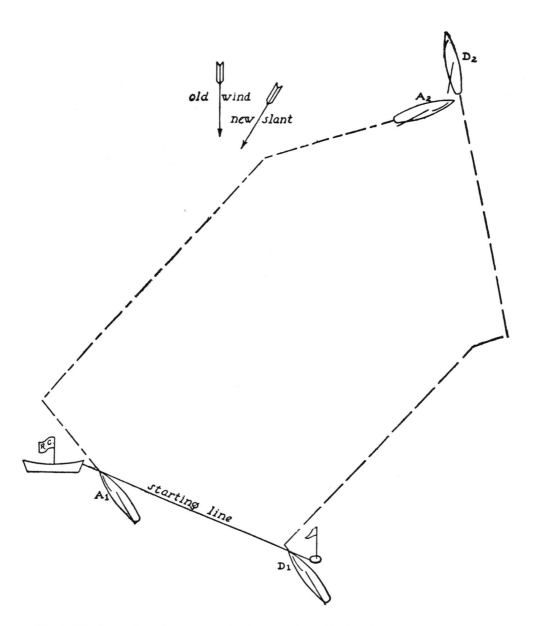

Fig. 26C—Boat A tacks eventually but too late. D, having gotten into the new slant first, takes the lead and might properly be considered to have gotten the start.

Boats of different sizes call for slightly different approaches at the start. Large boats need a long time to gain headway and, therefore, it is advisable for them to make a long run for the line, two minutes or thereabouts. This requires accurate timing. When making such a long run, one cannot always hope to hit the gun but, in a large boat, it is far better to be a couple of lengths late, and traveling fast, than on the line without much headway. Proper timing, however, can reduce the lateness to a minimum. By several trial approaches, carefully recording the length of time you sailed away from the line, allowing the proper number of seconds it takes to tack and then gain way again after heading back toward the line, an error of more than a few seconds should be (but all too often is not) exceptional.

Medium sized boats, such as Six-Metres or One-Tonners, attain good headway in 30 to 45 seconds. A fresh wind and smooth sea reduces this time, while a lump sea and dying breeze make it more difficult to gather way. Obviously, though, a long run is unnecessary and the boats should hover near the line, seldom more than one minute away during the whole preparatory period, jockeying constantly for position and using only the last thirty seconds or so for gathering way. Dinghies and light planing boats should stay nearer still, getting almost on the line well ahead of the gun in a favorable spot and luffing to stay there.

In all types of boats it is essential to create a gap to leeward of you to avoid being backwinded.

The Approach Course

Many starting tactics apply to yachts and classes of all sizes. On a windward start, we have noted that it is well to approach on the starboard tack unless the port tack favors tremendously. Furthermore, it is desirable to ease sheets just a few inches and give her a good rap full to gather way but, whenever possible, avoid reaching for the line or barging around the marker. In either of these cases, you have forfeited your right of way and may be disqualified even before the race has actually begun. (Fig. 27).

If the first leg is a run, the start, though less important, is still a big factor. Everyone knows that a boat will usually reach faster than she will run and, therefore, it is amazing how few people approach a dead run line on a reach, with the intention of squaring away with the gun. Such an approach has the double advantage of giving right of way over the dead running boats and a definite increase in speed. If the boats are on different tacks, the starboard tack boat will have right of way; if they are converging on the same jibe, the closer reaching boat, being closer to the wind and to leeward (because if to windward she would not be converging) has right of way over the other and can maintain her course. (Fig. 28).

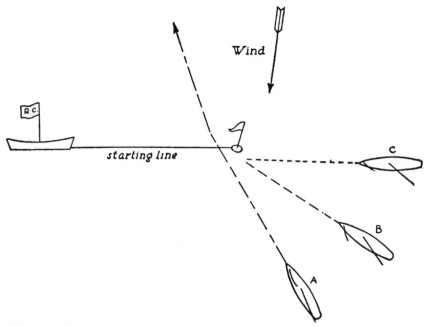

Fig. 27—Boats B and C are barging. Under the new rules, they can never claim room from A at the windward starting marker and must either pass the wrong side of the mark and restart or kill headway sufficiently for B to go astern of A and C astern of both.

One mistake which is frequently made in down wind starts is to drop the headsails and start under main alone. Although this has the advantage of speeding the spinnaker setting it is inadvisable, since the boat maneuvers poorly without a jib and, if a reaching approach is to be made (as I hope it will be), the under-canvassed boat cannot attain nearly so high a speed.

Follow a Set Plan

When the race is about to begin, the intense excitement of yachting's most thrilling moment and the crush of boats is apt to make the skipper forget all his well laid plans and force him to sail haphazardly through the fleet, looking at random for an opening. This is disastrous. Make sure that your boat has the right of way and then stick to the plan that had seemed rational in a calmer moment, making the other boats get out of your way and deviating from your plan only when it is absolutely necessary. Just following the fleet will seldom

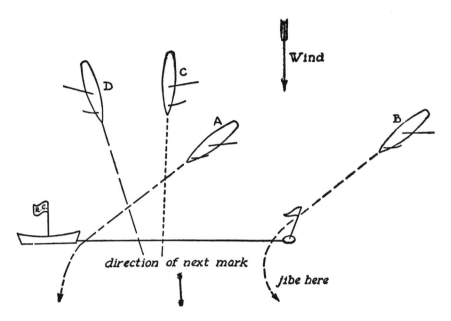

Fig. 28—Boats A and B are getting good starts. D is worst of
all. Why?

give you the number one spot. If you have planned to be early and loaf to
within thirty seconds sailing time of the line, then do it. By tacking in front of
the fleet and slacking sheets, one can maintain position close to the line (but
not so close that good headway cannot be gained before the gun fires) and still
make good starts. The overtaking and the windward boats must keep clear
and only the leeward ones which have gained an overlap need cause concern.
In other words, a boat in this spot, so long as she keeps clear of the leeward
boats, has rights which enable her to maintain her position and start as the
skipper had planned. If you have planned to stay behind the fleet and sail
through with full way at the last moment, don't let anyone force you close
sooner than you had planned. This method is more risky since, by becoming
the overtaking boat, you have forfeited many of your rights and may be
unable to find an opening. Either method can result in excellent starts but can
do so consistently only if you have practiced and planned in advance. If the
method you outlined was a good one and you keep your wits about you and
live up to your plan (and this becomes easier with every successive attempt)
then you will be getting good starts with surprising regularity. Of course, if
weather conditions change or something unexpected turns up at the last moment, it may be necessary to alter your plans abruptly and start as best befits
the new situation. Otherwise, have the courage of your earlier convictions;
don't be disturbed because the fleet is doing something else, and go to it.

Match Race Starts

Match races present a different problem altogether. In this case, regardless of the size of the boat, the emphasis should be placed on getting a better start than the other fellow. If, by getting a late start you can legally force your opponent into a worse one, then by all means do it. If you are a minute late but he is a minute and a quarter late, you have an excellent start, a far better one and often more skillful than if you had hit the line on the gun with the other boat only five seconds behind. As soon as three or more boats are involved, these tactis are, of course, invalid; while you are forcing one opponent into a late start, another may be stealing the show from both of you.

Match racing, including starting, is really an art in itself, which will be discussed at length in Chapter XVII.

Try to Be Early

When all is said and done, however, there is one cure for almost all poor starters, so simple it seems ridiculous even to mention it but so effective that it must be mentioned. Make up your mind to get over a few seconds earlier than you think you should. A poor starter is almost always late. It is the good ones that occasionally slip up and get over too early. It is natural to think you are over long before you are, so don't be afraid to call it close. You will be amazed to find that, even then, you seldom get over too early; though it is always well to look and listen for recall signals just to be sure. A former commodore of a well-known racing club once said: "I always try to get over ahead of time but damn it, I haven't succeeded yet." He was a good starter.

Don't be gun shy and, after you have had the thrill of leading the fleet across the starting line, remember that you are already well on your way to receiving the far greater thrill of leading them home across a different line in the other direction.

VII

Racing to Windward

ON BOTH WINDWARD and leeward and on triangular courses, more races are won and lost on the windward than on any other leg. On it there is less need to follow the leader and, consequently, greater opportunity for a wide variety of tactics whereby a skipper's skill, or lack of it, soon shows itself.

Behind the sailor who leads consistently at the weather mark are years of racing experience, but behind all the fine points at his command are a few basic rules and tactics which may be discussed here along with a few of the finer points. Knowing when to employ which rules and how to modify them to fit a particular race comes mainly with experience, but we shall try to shed some light on that aspect, too.

Racing a boat to windward successfully depends, first, on getting the most out of the boat (sailing her fast), and, second, on the use of proper tactics (sailing the fastest course). Only by a combination of the two can a race be won in keen competition.

GETTING THE MOST OUT OF THE BOAT

Assuming that a boat is properly tuned, sailing her fast to windward is dependent first and foremost on pointing properly.

Point Neither too High nor too Low

Pointing refers to the angle between the course a boat is steering and the direction of the wind. If a boat is beating to windward with a small angle between her course and the wind's direction she is pointing high. If there is a large angle between the direction she is heading and that of the wind, she is pointing low. (Fig. 29).

Pointing as high as possible enables a boat to head more nearly toward the windward mark. But, although she may be sailing the most direct and short-

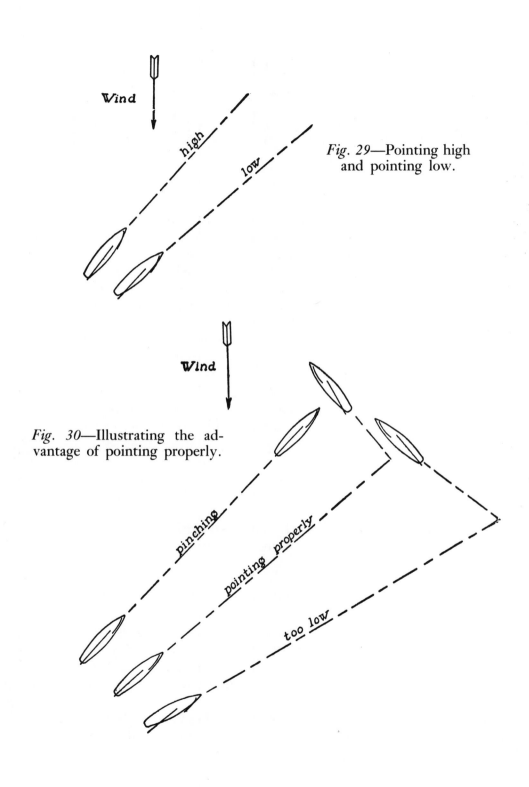

Wind

high

low

Fig. 29—Pointing high and pointing low.

Wind

Fig. 30—Illustrating the advantage of pointing properly.

pinching

pointing properly

too low

est course, she will not go as fast as a boat which bears off a bit. The latter will sail a longer course but may travel enough faster to reach the mark first. The best solution is to head neither too high nor too low; low enough so as not to "pinch" or "starve" the boat and so that she feels alive and goes fast but not so low that her added speed is more than offset by the additional distance she must cover. (Fig. 30).

How can we tell when we are pointing properly? Primarily it is a matter of feel. A boat that is sailing too close to the wind feels dead and sluggish. She lacks power to drive through seas and she often does not heel quite as much as usual. The sluggish sensation can be felt by the entire crew but, since it is transmitted through the tiller, is especially apparent to the skipper. He should hold the tiller with his fingers, not grab it with his palm. This light touch permits him to feel the action of the water against the rudder and the tiller becomes the nerve center of the boat's well being. It is difficult to describe the feel of a boat that is right but it is not difficult for an experienced skipper to recognize. The helm remains light yet it is not buffeted by each passing wave. The water can be felt rushing by. As a rule he doesn't analyze why she feels right. He just knows that she does.

Avoid Over Steering

A helmsman must be wary of steering too much. The action of waves and sudden puffs requires some movement of the tiller to keep the boat on her course, but don't try to fight her if she yaws momentarily. The next sea will probably bring her back. If it does not, a gentle movement of the tiller is sufficient. Continual working or sculling of the tiller may result in a slightly straighter course but it may also result in over correcting, so that the reverse is the case, and it creates unnecessary resistance. A well balanced boat will cling closely to the right course and needs only minimum guidance. She will almost sail herself to windward. Don't give her her head completely but do give her a chance.

The Use of Wind Pennants

A masthead fly or shroud telltales give an approximate indication of whether or not the boat is pointing properly. They should be *approximately* in the same vertical plane as the main boom—actually trailing off a bit more to leeward. A pennant's greatest value, however, is to indicate major wind shifts. Yarn sewn into the jib a few inches aft of the luff will prove very effective in telling when your boat is in the groove. If too high the yarn to windward will curl. If too low the yarn to leeward will curl. When just right both yarns stream straight along the sail.

Watch Competitors

Competitors give a good indication of whether you are pointing too high. If another boat, pointing a good bit higher than you are, is traveling about as fast, the chances are that you are too low. If, on the other hand, a competitor passes you and appears to be pointing very little lower, you are probably pinching. Bear off a bit and see if your boat does not feel better and go faster.

Certain types of boats can point higher than others. A centerboarder, because of her wide beam, usually must head lower than a keel boat to get good results. A deep narrow keel boat can point higher than a beamy, shoal draft one. Gaff rigs generally are not close winded. A Marconi rig is, especially if the aspect ratio is high.

In smooth water, a boat can point high and still carry way. In a sea, she must be put off a bit in order to gain added power to drive through. In light air, pointing a bit low produces best results. In stronger breezes, especially if the sea is not excessive, she should be "feathered" up to windward as much as possible.

The Trim of Sails

Proper trim of sails while beating is almost as important as pointing properly. If the boat feels dead, try slacking both main and jib *a few inches* and see if she doesn't perk up. In light air, best results are achieved if the sheets are eased a bit to give the sails more draft. Keep them full at all times. You won't point so high but you will sail a great deal faster. In stronger winds, both main and jib may be trimmed down considerably. The jib should always be trimmed flat and kept full even in very heavy winds. In heavy weather it might be advisable to slack the main a bit, carrying a big luff in it in order to keep the boat on her feet, and relying mostly on the jib for driving power.

Keep the Boat Heeling Only Slightly

In later chapters we will go into the problem of sailing in light and heavy winds in greater detail. Even at the risk of repetition, however, it seems wise to point out here that the boat should be heeling a bit while going to windward. In light air, place some of the crew weight to leeward, so gravity can help keep the sail full. In a breeze, put the weight as far to weather as possible, to keep the boat more nearly upright. The more common and more serious fault is to heel too much rather than too little.

Rap Full after Tacking

In the chapter on training the crew, we discussed the procedure for tacking. It should be added here that, after the tack has been completed, it is essential to get the boat back up to speed as soon as possible. This may be achieved best by slacking the sheets slightly and bearing off a little. As soon as she feels alive again (in a few lengths), trim down and point up as before. Sail the boat around rather than turn her quickly. A slow tack conserves momentum while a quick tack wastes it. This is particularly true of keel boats.

Keep Crew Low

While beating to windward it is especially important to keep the crew low. Even a head exposed to the wind can cause considerable harmful windage. If it is necessary for the crew to get out on the windward rail to increase stability, have them lie down and keep low. In smaller boats it is preferable for the crew and skipper to hike rather than lie out. The added stability from hiking more than offsets the windage. Star class sailors used to lie out, but you never see them do it now.

Position of Centerboard while Beating

In centerboard boats, the board should be all the way down, or nearly so, while beating to windward. This provides the required lateral resistance and prevents the boat from sliding off to leeward excessively. In boats which have pivoting boards, as opposed to a dagger type, the board can and should be manipulated to achieve better balance. If, with the board all the way down, there is excessive weather helm, try pulling it up a bit. This reduces the area hardly at all but does swing it aft. (Fig. 31). This in turn moves the center of lateral resistance aft and reduces the amount of weather helm. After a bit of experimenting with the board, the skipper can feel when she is right. Mark the pennant with twine or a dab of paint at that spot and lower exactly to the mark whenever similar wind conditions exist.

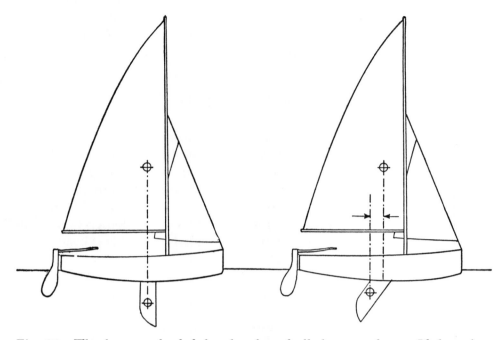

Fig. 31—The boat at the left has her board all the way down. If there is a weather helm, pulling the board up, as in the boat at the right, moves the center of lateral resistance aft of the center of force exerted on the sails. This in turn will remove or reduce weather helm and achieve balance.

TACTICS

Usually of even greater importance than sailing a boat at high speed to windward is the use of proper tactics. By this we mean going the right place, hindering your competitors by fair methods and eluding their interference. Tactics vary in each race and with each changing set of conditions, but many apply frequently and these have the greatest bearing on success.

Avoid Excess Tacking

In a steady wind, it is advisable to avoid frequent tacking while sailing the windward leg. Each time a boat goes about she loses headway and loses time in regaining it. In a shifting wind, when covering a competitor or when forced to clear one's wind, frequent tacking may be justified. Otherwise, it makes sense to reach the weather mark on two or three long tacks, going about a minimum number of times. Weigh each decision to tack against the positive loss of 15 to 100 feet, depending upon the size of the boat, and the condition of wind and sea.

Which Tack to Take?

As the windward leg begins, we must decide on the initial tack. Other things being equal, it is safer to take the one which heads more nearly toward the mark. The mark is often not dead to windward and, by choosing the tack which brings us closest to it, we are less apt to be affected adversely if the

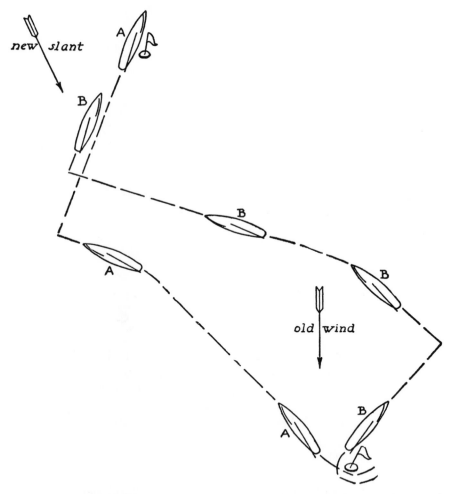

Fig. 32A—Boat A chooses the tack which heads nearest the mark. Upon being headed, she is able to come about and cross B easily.

wind does shift. Should we then be let up we might lay the mark. If headed, we can come about to advantage. The boat which went about on the short leg to begin with is little or no nearer to the mark than when she started. If the wind lets her up after she has come about to head for the mark, she will have overstood. If headed, she will have to tack again to fetch the mark. (Figs. 32A and 32B).

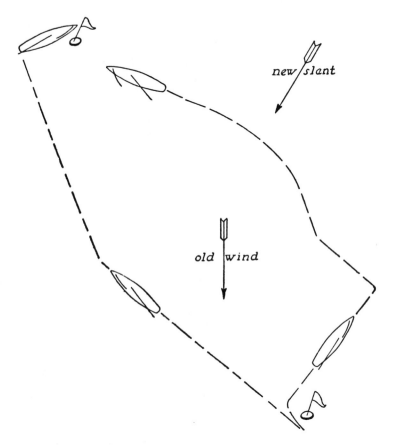

Fig. 32B—In this case, A again takes the tack heading nearest the mark. When the wind lets her up, she almost lays it. The new slant merely causes B to overstand.

Sail in the Direction of Expected Wind Shifts

Many conditions govern the choice of which tack to take. For example, if a wind shift, even a small one, is expected, start in the direction from which the shift will originate. In other words, sail toward wind slants which will head you on your original tack. Then when you are headed you can come about and will point much higher on the new tack. (Fig. 33).

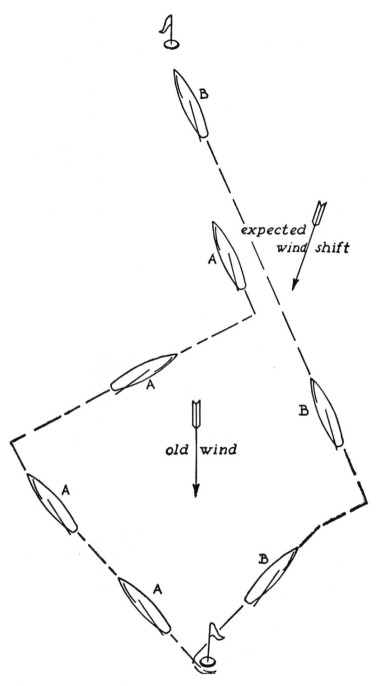

Fig. 33—Boat B, by tacking toward an expected wind shift, gains on A.

The same rule applies when heading for stronger winds, even if there is no attending shift in direction. By reaching the stronger wind first, you are almost sure to gain.

An exception to the rule of sailing toward wind shifts exists if you can almost lay the mark and expect a let-up. Here the tactic of sailing the course which takes you nearest to the mark has precedence.

Predicting Wind Shifts

"All very well," you might say, "but how do I know how the wind will shift and how can I tell where it is apt to blow the hardest?" Sometimes, in fluky going, you simply do not know and cannot know. At such times, it is often best to go about each time a header is encountered, thus always keeping on the tack taking you nearest to the mark. But more often there are indications to guide you.

The Use of Smoke

One of these may be smoke from a chimney or fire ashore, or from a passing steamer. By watching the direction it is trailing you can gauge the direction of the wind in that locality. Smoke also indicates strength of wind. If it is laying out flat there is considerable wind. Experience will teach you to determine whether it is a stronger wind than the one you have where you are. If the smoke spirals lazily upward, there is little wind. Remember, however, that if the smoke is coming from a steamer, it is necessary to allow for her movement in figuring both strength and direction of the wind. This is difficult but it can be done.

Learn from Other Boats

Other boats in your own or other classes frequently give a tip-off of new wind slants. If distant boats are heeling more than those near you, it is a safe bet that they have a stronger wind. By watching how they are heading on various tacks, and comparing same to your own course, an accurate estimate of their wind's direction can be made.

Recognize Wind on the Water

Often, new and stronger slants appear as a darker line on the water. All of the above signs can be read more accurately with a good pair of marine glasses. Every racing boat should have a pair on board. They are useful for finding marks, reading course signals, etc. If your crew is large enough and includes an experienced racing man, it is advisable to have him spend the entire windward leg looking for such signs. You will want to look, too, and probably you will make the final decision but two heads, and especially another pair of eyes, are better than one. Such an arrangement has the added advantage of allowing the helmsman to concentrate on sailing the boat.

Note the Wind Direction in Puffs

Another hint can often be gathered from puffs. If the wind changes direction in a puff, there is a better than even chance that if it does shift permanently it will coincide with the direction encountered in these puffs. Sometimes a new slant comes in at first only in spots rather than on a broad front and a strong wind is apt to prevail over a lighter one.

Study Cloud Formations

Cloud formations, such as thunderheads or mares' tails, may give valuable dope on new winds. As a rule, when a thunderhead makes up, the new wind can be expected to blow from its direction.

Even without any of the indications discussed thus far, it may be possible to predict wind shifts with a reasonable degree of accuracy. In our discussion of the morning of the race, we advised calling the weather bureau to learn of impending changes in the wind and weather. Keep that information in the back of your mind, but don't give it undue importance unless local signs tend to corroborate it or unless you have no other indications to go on.

Local Knowledge

Of greater assistance is local knowledge. Wind has a habit of shifting according to a known pattern in various localities. On Western Long Island Sound, for example, in a light and spotty easterly wind, there is every reason to expect a southerly to come off the Long Island shore late in the afternoon. Under these conditions many of the keener skippers take a course to put them in the most advantageous position should the southerly materialize. It is remarkable how many races are won by making use of this knowledge.

Somewhat akin to local knowledge, except that it applies universally, is the fact that wind usually hauls off a beach. Frequently, as a boat nears the shore she gets headed and can "make money" by coming about on the other tack. The effect of current can also be a big factor in deciding on the best windward course. This we will treat at greater length in a separate chapter.

Especially in a heavy sea, it is often advisable to take a tack which will put you in the lee of a shore. Not only is the wind apt to haul off the shore, but it is not so rough there and boats travel considerably faster in smooth water.

Luck or Instinct?

The suggestions we have made here for choosing the best tack are not quite the whole story. An experienced skipper can often "guess" where to go. Of course, it isn't really a guess but is based on past experience. Ask him why he chose a certain tack and he may say he doesn't really know—"just thought it would be best." When these "guesses" pay off a majority of the time, one begins to realize that they are a great deal more than luck. Luck can be a factor and a big one for one race, less often for a series, seldom for a year. A skipper cannot be lucky year after year.

Sailing fast and choosing the fastest course is by no means the whole story of racing to windward. The primary object is to get around the course ahead of every other boat, rather than in the shortest time. It follows, therefore, that tactics are governed by your position in relation to other boats in the fleet.

We will assume at first that yours is the leading boat.

Stay Between the Fleet and the Mark

One of the cardinal rules to be observed by leading boats is to stay between the fleet and the next mark. Doing so is the conservative course and, if your lead is sufficient, you may be able to short tack up the middle, covering the entire fleet to some extent, and still beat the boats which took long port or starboard tacks. At least you will be assured of beating most of the boats and thus will preserve your series average.

Cover Nearest Competitors

If you are the leading boat of several which are well ahead of the bulk of the fleet, it is best to stay between these nearest boats and the mark. Probably the rest of the fleet will not catch up and your best chance of winning lies in turning back the challenge of those which threaten most closely.

When not to Cover?

Under certain circumstances, it may be wiser not to cover either the fleet or the nearest boats. Instead, you may want to concentrate on sailing the fastest course. This will tend to force your nearest competitors to split tacks and, if you were correct in your selection of a course, you are sure to win.

When should this admittedly risky procedure be followed? Certainly in the early stages of the race, when your lead is slight. Under these conditions the most conservative action and the safest one, if your judgment is good, is to sail your own race. Choose what seems to be the best course and let the rest go hang. You have every advantage. Your wind is free and you can go anywhere you desire. After you have worked out a fairly comfortable lead of 100 yards or more, and only then, it is time to think of covering either the fleet or your nearest pursuers. It usually costs distance to cover and it is unwise to do so until you can afford to lose something and still stay in front. Overconservatism is as costly as excessive chance taking. Don't feel sorry for the skipper who complains about being ahead at the start and who covered the fleet "according to all the rules" yet was beaten by several boats that "took a flyer" off to one side. Chances are, he covered too soon and should have been "taking a flyer" himself.

Usually, if you have a slow boat, it is advisable not to cover either the fleet or your nearest competitor prior to the very late stages of the race. Superior judgment has gotten you ahead and that alone can keep you there. Only by sailing the fastest course, and forcing your nearest competitors to take a slower one, can you stay on top.

Cutting Boats Behind

One of the advantages of being ahead is that you have the ability to cut the boats behind, thus slowing them down. This is a perfectly fair procedure and those who complain loudest would doubtless do the same to you were they able. Cutting, or blanketing, refers to taking a boat's wind. It is done when your sail is between hers and the direction the *apparent* wind is coming from. This reduces the amount of wind she gets and will certainly slow her down. (Fig. 34).

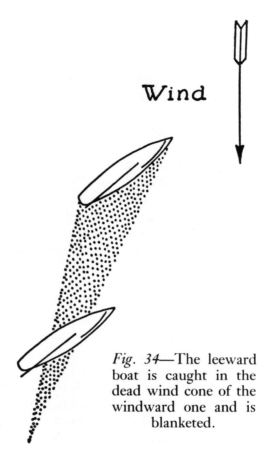

Fig. 34—The leeward boat is caught in the dead wind cone of the windward one and is blanketed.

The Safe Leeward Position

Akin to cutting is backwinding through the safe leeward position. This refers to a boat which is ahead and slightly to leeward of another. The wind striking the leading boat's sails is deflected against the leeward side of the other's sails. The trailing boat finds herself unable to point as high, her sails go aback slightly and she slows down. It is almost impossible to pass a boat that has attained the safe leeward position, hence its name. (Fig. 35). The quarter wave of the leeward boat is also an obstacle the windward boat cannot ride over.

To Cut or not to Cut

It is not always to the leading boat's advantage to cut or blanket those astern, either directly or through backwind in the safe leeward position. In a

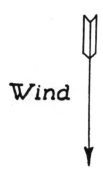

Wind

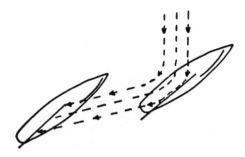

Fig. 35—The wind, striking the sails of the leading boat, is deflected aft and backwinds the trailing boat. The leader is in the safe leeward position.

match race, cut at every opportunity. Also, in the late stages of a race, when only one competitor is threatening, cut him all you can. It is also advisable to cut a boat at any time when you are virtually certain that you are on the right tack. If he splits tacks to clear his wind he will sail a less desirable course. Cut, also, if your boat is slower than your pursuer's. There may be no other way to stay ahead.

At other times it may be better to give your nearest competitor a clear wind. If you do, he will probably sail the same course you are and, unless he is faster, you should stay ahead. If you do cut him, he may split tacks, which puts you in a quandary whether to cover him or not. Each time you tack to cover, you lose distance on the rest of the fleet. You will doubtless stay ahead of the nearest boat but in the process others may sail by. And it makes the other skipper sore if you cut him repeatedly *without good reason* and he may do the same to you if he gets ahead.

If you do want to cut a boat and can just cross her bow, is it better to take a safe leeward position or cross and tack on top of her? The answer varies depending on the proximity of the mark but as a rule the safe leeward position is preferable. If you skin across her bow and then tack, she may be able to break through your lee before you have regained full headway and may get a safe leeward position on you. By tacking on her lee bow, you are farther ahead

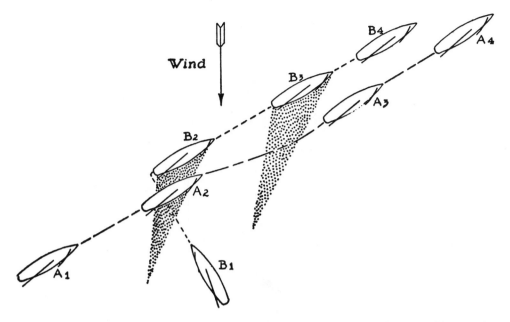

Fig. 36A—Boat B crosses A and tacks to cover. Upon completion of her tack, she is cutting A. But B has not gained headway and A increases hers by rapping slightly. This enables her to break clear of B's wind shadow and, by feathering up, she may gain the safe leeward position and draw ahead of B.

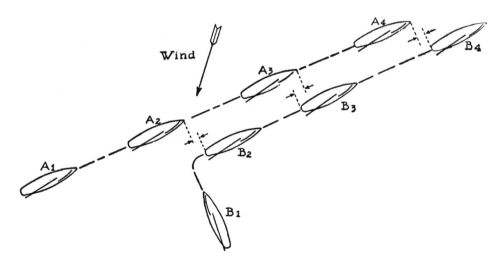

Fig. 36B—This time, B tacks short of A, loses some ground at first but gains the safe leeward position. A is unable to clear her wind except by tacking and drops astern.

when you do come about and it is much harder for her to pass while you are gaining way. (Figs. 36A and 36B).

If behind, what tactics are recommended?

Get Your Wind Clear

The first and foremost rule when cut or backwinded is to get your wind clear. Don't delay. Either take a short tack to clear it or ease sheets and attempt to break through the lee of the boat or boats that are cutting you.

Once your wind is clear, the question arises whether to split tacks with the boats ahead or attempt to sail by them. If you have a fast boat, the latter course is recommended. If the leaders appear to be sailing a poor course, you are in luck. Split tacks at once and sail the course which seems best. If, as is more often the case, all conditions point to the fact that the leaders are sailing the right course, it is best to plug along after them, even if you haven't got a faster boat. This is hard medicine to swallow. Many other boats, finding it too tough to take, may split tacks. Then, if your judgment was correct, it won't be long before you have passed them and gained a good position, even though not in the lead. In a series, this practice is recommended even more strongly. It may result in fewer wins but it preserves an average. Furthermore, by plugging after the leaders who are sailing the best course, you will be near enough to capitalize on any mistakes or bad breaks they may encounter. In this way, you might even win. Never say die, for the race is never over until the finish.

If hopelessly behind, and your boat is no faster or slower than the others, your only hope is to take a flyer and get off by yourself. When doing this, be sure to go far enough. Nothing is gained by half-way measures. Once off by yourself, there is always a chance of getting an unexpected slant which will bring you home a winner. Races are won that way and it isn't altogether luck when they are.

In fact, there is less luck and more skill required on windward legs than on any other. When first at the weather mark, you have done something. The race may be far from won but it is a great satisfaction to be out in front when the slide down-hill begins.

VIII

Racing to Leeward

WHILE THE WINDWARD leg is pretty generally conceded to be the most important one, the leading boat at the windward mark by no means has the race in
her pocket. In a triangular race, two of the legs are off wind; while on a
windward-leeward course half the distance is covered while running free.
This affords considerable distance in which to improve one's position and
there are countless methods for doing so.

As in racing to windward, the problem may be divided into parts; first
increase the boat's speed and, second (and perhaps more important), the use of
tactics for sailing the best course and hindering one's competitors.

INCREASING SPEED OFF WIND

Weight Distribution

Changes in weight distribution to maintain the boat's best fore and aft trim
are necessary when the leeward legs begin. In a strong breeze, crew weight
should be moved a bit aft. Under such conditions, the wind's pressure against
the sails buries the bow and this tendency must be offset. In light airs, moving
the crew forward is sometimes in order, especially if your boat has a broad,
flat stern which is apt to cause drag. The exact weight distribution varies for
boats of different type but it is seldom indeed that some changes from the fore
and aft trim which proved fastest to windward are not necessary. A bit of
experimenting will soon indicate the required alteration. Watch your competitors closely to gain information on the relative performance of your own
boat.

Location of weight athwartships is likewise important. On a reach, the
boat should heel to leeward *very slightly*. It is important, especially while
reaching in strong winds, to keep her "on her feet" with the crew well up to
windward. While running, most boats sail best when on an even keel. In a

84

dinghy or any beamy boat with a cat rig, it is good practice (except perhaps in very light winds) to heel the boat slightly to windward in order to offset the thrust to windward which the off-center position of the sail makes. With more of the windward than the leeward half of the bottom immersed in the water, the resulting asymmetrical form of the underwater shape of the boat combats this thrust, reduces weather helm and increases speed. The most general error, both when running and reaching, is to sail with too great an angle of heel.

Windage is unimportant while sailing off wind and hence the crew may sit on deck where the sails can be worked most easily.

It is important, when considering both athwartships and fore and aft trim, to remember that, when one crew member goes forward or to leeward, his weight should be compensated by another moving aft or to windward. As far as possible, however, without hindering working efficiency, the crew should be concentrated close together near the spot that will provide the fastest trim to the hull, toward the center when sailing upwind, and further aft when going downwind. The crew should never be spread widely forward and aft, where their weight can cause the boat to hobbyhorse.

Changes in Sheet Leads

When reaching, sheet leads of headsails should be moved out and aft. This permits the clew of the jib, genoa or ballooner to flow out more to leeward. The foot of the sail then follows a smooth curve instead of hooking in sharply to the fairlead position used while beating. It also allows the sail to lift more. Both factors increase the drive immeasurably. (Fig. 37).

Many boats have sliding leads to permit adjustment. On others, separate leads must be used. In the latter case, the weather jib sheet may be brought around and passed through this new lead. The strain on the jib is then shifted to this lead. In a small boat, it is often possible to improve the sheet position still further by holding it out to leeward by hand. The racing rules forbid outriggers or whisker poles for this purpose but do not outlaw manual means.

Proper Trim

While running or reaching, sheets should be slacked as far as they will go without causing the sails to luff. Keep them full but always on the verge of a break. Slack out occasionally until the first sign of a luff is noticed; then trim back a few inches. Continuous working of the sheets is essential. A wind

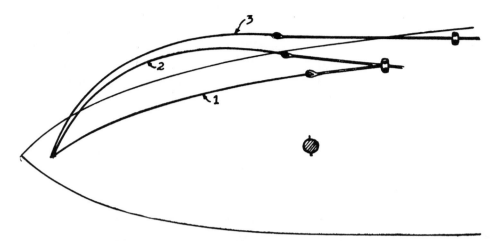

Fig. 37—Lead #1 shows the shape of the jib when led correctly for beating. If the same lead is used on a reach, the jib hooks in too much, as in #2. A lead farther aft and outboard results in the smooth curve of draft seen in #3.

pennant and shroud telltales are useful in determining when the proper trim has been gained without having to luff to find out. Woolies (wool yarn telltales) attached to both sides of the jib approximately 10″ to 12″ from the luff are also most helpful. When the windward one is curling, you should trim. When the leeward one curls, you should ease. When both are streaming, your trim is correct. It is on off wind sailing that a wind pennant really justifies its use. When running dead before it, the main boom should be slacked off nearly at right angles to the wind and the spinnaker boom squared until it is about in line with the main boom (actually a bit forward). The spinnaker sheet should be slacked well out so that the sail can flow around the headstay and out ahead, away from the dead air behind the main. The most common fault when sailing to leeward is to trim all sails too flat. It is a neat trick to keep them always close to a luff and still full, but it can be done.

In a strong breeze, weather helm may be reduced by slacking the main so that it luffs. This has the further advantage of keeping the boat more nearly upright. No boat can go fast when she is over on her ear and fighting a strong weather helm. In a heavy breeze she goes much faster with as much as half the main aback (even more in extreme conditions). The jib remains full and, aided by the after part of the main, drives her at top speed. In very heavy air you will go faster by having a luff in the top part of the jib. This can be done by moving the jib lead well aft.

Remember not to trim too flat and to sail your boat on her bottom not her side.

Use of a Boom Vang

Closely related to proper trim of the mainsail is the use of a boom vang or guy. This is a tackle, on a small boat, a line, one end of which is attached to the boom slightly forward of its mid-point, with the other end leading to the foot of the mast or as near thereto as feasible. (Fig. 38). When the leeward leg begins, except in light airs, a heavy strain is taken on this tackle. Its advantages are many. The chief one is the added drive given to the upper part of the sail. This is particularly true of tall, narrow sails. The vang keeps the boom low and in the process prevents the upper leech from sagging off to leeward. Both upper and lower halves of the sail thus remain in approximately the same plane. As a result, it is possible to slack the boom further without causing a luff aloft. Without a vang, in order to keep the upper half of the sail full and driving, the lower half must be trimmed too flat for best speed. (Fig. 39).

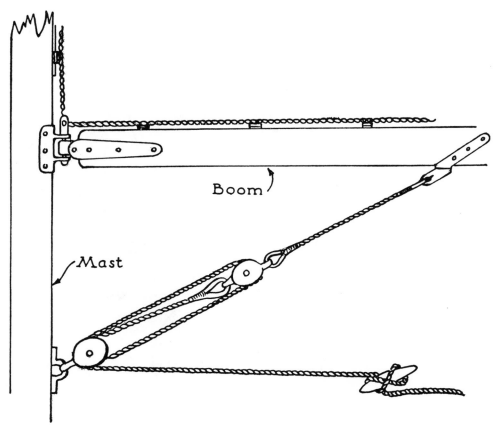

Fig. 38—A typical rig for a boom vang.

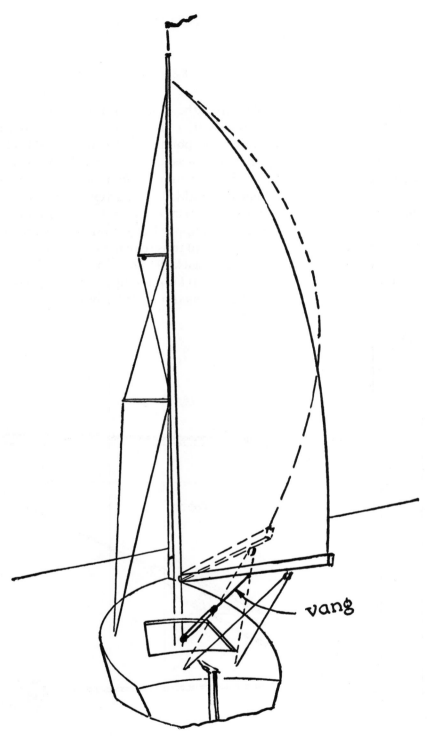

Fig. 39—Illustrating how the use of a boom vang permits a more uniform shape throughout the length of the sail and increases drive aloft. The dotted line indicates a sail with no vang.

The sail may be slacked and trimmed without changing the vang. It holds the boom *down* rather than *in*. Of all the effective devices for increasing speed down wind, none is more important than the boom vang. On many larger boats a hydraulic vang is used instead of a tackle, and on others a tackle is led to a semicircular track, or to padeyes on deck, rather than to the foot of the mast, thus permitting a more direct and efficient downward pull. Whatever type you have, be sure to use it. In light air, trimming it too hard might make the main too flat. And in *very* heavy air you might want to ease the vang somewhat in order to reduce heeling. In moderate to fresh air it should be trimmed hard. Make your vang plenty strong, as the strain on it will be considerable.

The vang is useful in both reaching and running. In the latter instance, it has the additional advantage of eliminating some of the disastrous effects of an accidental jibe. It will not prevent the jibe but will keep the boom from cocking up in the air and striking the permanent backstay.

Special Down Wind Sails

The most obvious and effective means of increasing speed down wind is by using additional sails. Few small boats carry balloon jibs, but those that do should break them out on close reaches except in very strong winds.

Far more common is the use of the spinnaker. While running, it is certainly the most effective sail and is almost as good on a reach until the wind draws more than a half point forward of the beam. Rod Stephens' advice, "when in doubt, carry your spinnaker," is well worth following. Properly designed and trimmed spinnakers may be used to good advantage when the true wind is abeam. In heavy weather, don't use it until the wind is well abaft the beam; in light airs, it may be carried with wind slightly forward of the beam. Remember that with the true wind abeam, the apparent wind is forward of the beam. The faster the boat's speed, the farther forward comes the direction of the apparent wind, and the greater becomes its strength. (Fig. 40). Flat, reaching type, spinnakers may be used on a slightly closer reach than the more common parachute but the latter is also effective for reaching. At all times give it all the sheet it will take, keeping the sail on the verge of breaking and with sheet led as far out and aft as possible. On a run, the lead may be further forward if desired. At all times, put your best man on the spinnaker sheet and have him play it continually.

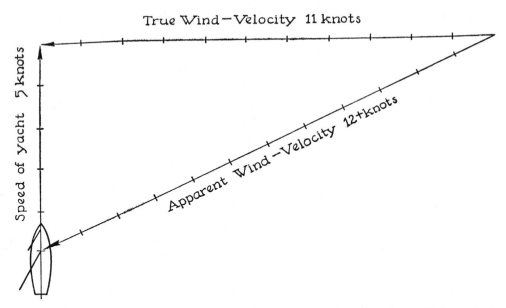

Fig. 40—Note how the boat's movement draws the direction of the wind farther forward. With wind abeam or forward of the beam it increases its strength also. With wind abaft the beam, it reduces the wind's strength.

Reduce Curve of Mast

Boats which have means for bending their spars should remove much of the curve when the leeward leg commences. We have already noted that this curve flattens the main and, on a reach or run, the mainsail should be as full as possible.

Position of Centerboard

Centerboard boats perform best off wind with part or all of their board hoisted. On a run, all of the board may be housed unless steering is difficult. On a close reach, only a little board should be brought up. By pulling it up slightly (and aft in the process, assuming yours is a pivoting board) weather helm is reduced and there is still enough surface left to prevent excessive leeway. On broader reaches, less board is required. Experimenting will show how much is needed; the amount varies on different boats. It should be lowered at least part way when rounding marks or in close quarters, to facilitate maneuvering.

Even more important are the down wind tactics.

Sail Toward Favoring Winds

As on windward legs, it is advisable to sail toward stronger winds and favoring slants. Unless the new breeze is considerably stronger than the one you already have, it is well not to sail far off the direct course for the next mark. But you can edge over toward the wind so that when it arrives your side of the fleet will get it first. In extreme cases, it may be worth while sailing as much as 45° off the course to reach it. But bear in mind that the additional distance thus sailed must be more than offset by a resulting increase in speed.

The stronger wind is not the only reason for sailing off the course. It is equally profitable to sail toward new slants which will give a more favorable sailing angle. A boat sails slower running than reaching. On a dead run, therefore, if a new slant off to one side will permit a reach for the next mark, it may be well worth a lot of extra distance to get into it. While heading toward the new breeze, you will be on a reach and upon arrival in the new wind, will be able to reach for the mark. Thus at all times you will be sailing faster than the boat running on the direct course. Especially in light airs, one might sail as much as one-third farther and yet reach the mark first. (Fig. 41).

Jibe on the Lifts

One of the most effective and overlooked tactics on a run is that of jibing on the lifts. Everyone knows the benefit one gains when sailing a windward leg by tacking in a header. It allows you to sail closer to the mark after tacking.

The same applies on a run. If it is a dead run to start with, and you get lifted, there is no way to head for the mark unless you jibe, and extra distance will be sailed. Furthermore, in your desire not to sail too far from the rhumb line, if you don't jibe you are apt to keep the wind too far aft, or even sail by the lee, thus reducing speed. Except in very heavy air you will have to tack downwind anyway, and by jibing on each lift you will always be on the fastest tack and sailing a shorter distance. Even if you are on a broad spinnaker reach and get lifted so that the only way you can keep heading for the mark is to run directly for it, it is preferable to jibe instead of either running for the mark or heading high on the initial tack. Most wind shifts are temporary, and by jibing in this situation you will get far enough away from the rhumb line so

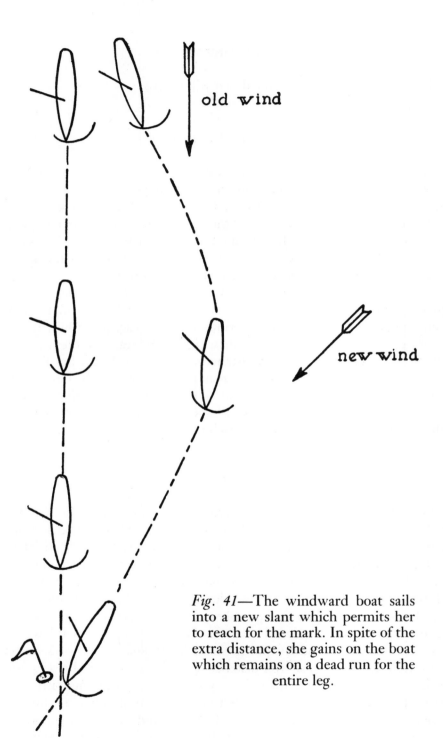

old wind

new wind

Fig. 41—The windward boat sails into a new slant which permits her to reach for the mark. In spite of the extra distance, she gains on the boat which remains on a dead run for the entire leg.

that when the wind does shift back you can jibe again to your original tack and have a really fast point of sailing to the mark. You will have strayed no farther from the rhumb line and sailed no greater distance than a boat that didn't jibe, but when the wind shifts back, he will be faced with a slow run to the mark while you will go like blazes with the wind well on your quarter. Again refer to Fig. 41.

To insure a fast sailing angle, coupled usually with a shorter distance sailed, jibing on the lifts is wonderfully effective. It becomes particularly effective because so many sailors seem to avoid jibes in fear of a foul-up, and also because so many others don't seem to recognize the tremendous gains that are possible through use of this tactic.

Tacking Down Wind

Even if the wind remains absolutely steady in direction, much the same is accomplished through tacking down wind, first broad reaching on one tack, then jibing over and broad reaching on the other. Greater distance is covered than when running directly for the mark but boats reach so much faster that it may be worth while. This will not work in strong winds (except in boats of planing type) when boats are close to their maximum speed. It works particularly well in light air, and the lighter the wind, the greater the angle at which you should tack downwind. In very light air it sometimes pays to sail so high as to bring the apparent wind on the beam. It also works best in boats which have small spinnakers unsuited to a dead run, but if conditions are right it can apply to all types. (Fig. 42).

Spotting New Winds

Stronger winds and changes in direction may be detected in the same fashion as when sailing to windward. Other boats, smoke, dark streaks on the water and local knowledge give the tip-off and remember to use your marine glasses.

Bear Off in Puffs

The knowledge that in light winds a boat broad reaches faster than she runs, and close reaches faster than she broad reaches, may be utilized to good advantage in another way. In between puffs, trim down a bit and head a point or so above the direct course. In the lighter air, this sharper angle will permit

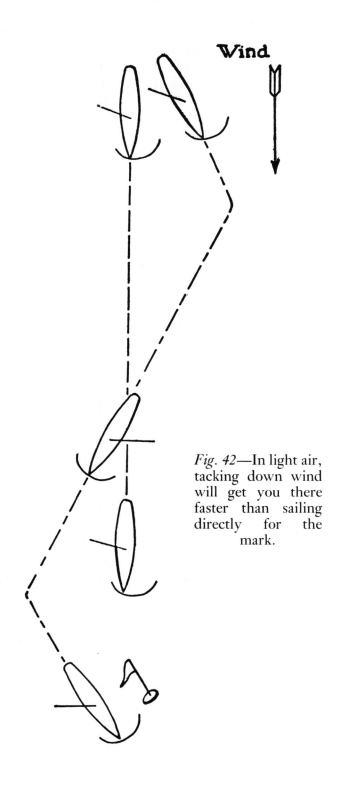

Wind

Fig. 42—In light air, tacking down wind will get you there faster than sailing directly for the mark.

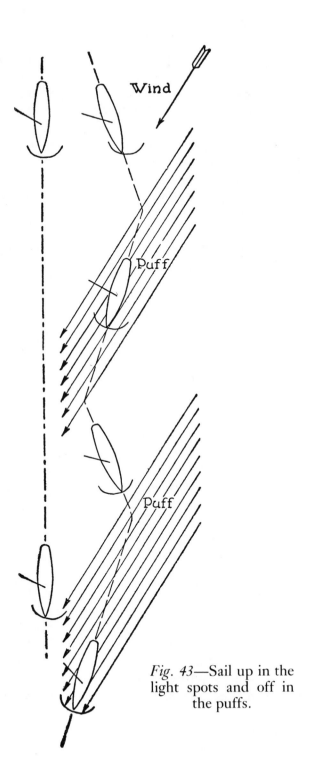

Wind

Puff

Puff

Fig. 43—Sail up in the light spots and off in the puffs.

sailing much faster and will *get you into the next puff sooner*. (Fig. 43). Whenever a puff is encountered, bear off a point or so below the base course. In the stronger wind you will go nearly as fast as if you had held your course, perhaps even faster in very strong winds, and, by sailing more in the direction the puff is traveling, you will *stay in it longer*. In this way, one *averages* the direct course, stays in the strong winds longer and sails faster than the boat on the direct course. True, the distance is a bit greater but it is more than offset by the higher speed. Not many skippers employ this tactic but the winners do to a greater or lesser extent. Its use cannot be recommended too highly.

In a dying breeze, it is well to sail low of the course in the early stages of the leg when the wind is strongest, so as to be able to reach up and sail fast in the latter part of the leg when the breeze has lightened. Conversely, in a rising breeze, reach up high of the course at first, thereby getting far enough ahead to be able to bear off later on in the stronger winds and still hold a lead.

Be Inside at the Mark

In selecting your course on a reach or run, plan ahead to be in the inside berth at the mark. In a later chapter we will go at some length into the subject of approaching and rounding marks but it is of sufficient importance to warrant mention here.

Tactics for the Leading Boats

If ahead, it is far easier to cover the fleet or your nearest competitors than it was on the windward leg. And usually it is wise to do so, sailing a middle course when covering the fleet or the course of the nearest pursuers if the bulk of the fleet is way behind. If the nearest boats appear to be sailing a poor course in a desperate gamble to pass, they should not be covered.

On a dead run or broad reach the leading boat must maneuver to avoid being blanketed by those behind, either by working up to windward or going far enough to leeward to keep a clear wind. Don't continue to work up to windward if those astern insist on going still higher. It may be slow going when you try to come down and you are liable to be blanketed as you square off for the mark. Consequently, it is apt to be best to let them go and try to keep your wind clear by getting far enough to leeward. If they threaten, you can usually stay in front by reaching up across their bows on a faster sailing angle.

Luffing matches are also of doubtful value, except in the very late stages of a race. Luffing will keep a faster boat astern for a while but not forever, and even if you are able to keep her from passing, the rest of the fleet may gain so much as to make it hardly worth while. In two-boat races, luffing matches are O.K.

Frequently, there is misunderstanding about the position in which one boat will cut or blanket another when sailing free. At first glance it appears that by getting directly between a boat and the direction the wind is coming from, the leeward or leading boat will be cut. *Such is not the case.* If both boats were stationary, it would be true, but since both are moving, the leeward or leading boat stays ahead of the blanket of dead air. Stated in other terms, the dead air does not stream directly to leeward of the windward boat because the boat's movement bends this blanketed section aft. It is for this reason that a boat apparently cut actually retains a clear wind. In order to blanket her, it is necessary to take a position which will compensate for the difference between the direction of the true wind and the axis of the cone of dead air. (Figs. 44A and 44B). Watch the other boat's sails to see when you are blanketing her.

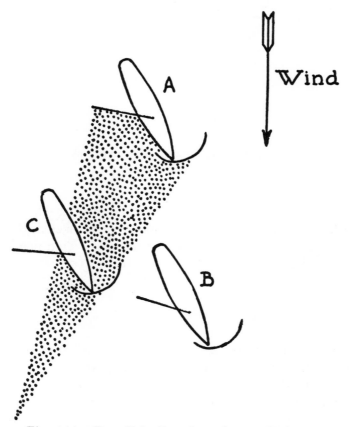

Fig. 44A—Boat B is directly to leeward of A but C
is being blanketed instead.

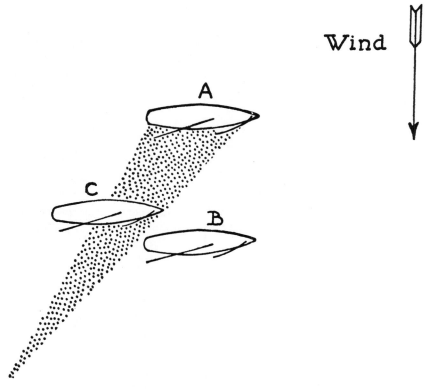

Fig. 44B—Once again, B is directly to leeward of A but keeps her
wind clear, while C is cut.

Since your masthead fly shows apparent wind direction, when it is pointing directly at a boat to leeward of you she should be blanketed. By the same
token, if you are the leeward boat and the other boat's wind pennant is not
trailing off in your direction, your wind is still clear.

Tactics for the Boat Behind

The boat astern on leeward legs is in a good position to profit by the
mistakes of the leaders. The nearest boats may be passed by getting in position to cut them but this only raises the danger of being blanketed subse-
quently by them, and hence is of doubtful value except just before the finish.

It is usually better to watch the course of the leaders and try to sail a faster
one. Often they allow themselves to be sucked up to windward to keep a clear
wind. There is your chance to ride the puffs down to leeward and reach
through when they try to come down in lighter going. You may also see the

leaders run into soft spots and be able to change course and pass either to windward or to leeward. Except in a steady wind, and then not entirely, leeward legs are far from the follow the leader procession that they are often considered.

If a windward leg is to follow and you are not hopelessly behind, it is apt to be wisest to follow the leaders, providing they appear to be steering a good course. By so doing, you will stay close enough to be in striking distance on the windward leg. If way behind, then a gamble is justified. Once you decide to take one, go far enough to one side or the other, to make it worth while.

If your boat is slow off wind, you may be able to keep up with a faster one by getting a few feet astern of her and following directly in her wake. If you get in the trough of one of her stern waves, she will carry you along. Riding her quarter wave sometimes achieves the same result. It is possible to "get a tow" in this manner from slightly faster boats in other classes. It will burn up your competitors if you pass them in this fashion, but to us it seems perfectly fair and it has been done.

Don't underestimate the importance of leeward legs.

IX

Handling the Spinnaker

IN OTHER CHAPTERS, the problems of sail handling have been touched on. Proper setting, trimming and dousing of the spinnaker, however, are important enough to warrant further consideration.

SETTING THE SPINNAKER

The observance of a few simple rules will greatly facilitate the task of spinnaker setting. It is helpful, for example, to have a swivel attached to the head of this sail. When hoisting, the spinnaker is apt to become twisted and a well oiled swivel removes almost all such chance. The use of a braided halliard helps further to prevent twisting the spinnaker while it is being hoisted in stops. The friction of a twisted rope running over a sheave or through a fairlead is sufficient to unlay the rope, causing a few turns in the sail. After the sail is broken out, if it is twisted after all, slacking away a foot or two on the halliard and then rehoisting smartly will usually clear it.

To Set Flying or in Stops?

If the spinnaker is set flying it can be made to draw sooner. Therefore, in all but boats of 50 feet and larger, or in very strong winds when there is a chance of the sail filling before being fully hoisted, it's preferable to set the spinnaker out of a box, bag, or turtle. This method will be discussed in the second half of this chapter under the heading "Small Boat Spinnaker Technique."

Mark Head, Tack and Clew

It will save time if identifying marks, either ink or a few turns of colored twine, or small swatches of colored cloth are put on the head, tack and clew of the spinnaker. This is especially true of single type spinnakers which are cut differently on leech and luff. Such a marking system permits positive and instant identification, saves time and removes the possibility of attaching a guy where the sheet or halliard should be, both of which have been done on my boat.

Hoisting

Before hoisting, overhaul the spinnaker to make sure it is free of twists and then attach the sheet, guys and halliard. The sail may also be attached to the outboard end of the pole. Some prefer to make this final attachment after the sail is hoisted. In any event, be sure to attach the after guy to the tack of the sail, not to the pole direct. (See Fig. 45). The pole is then snapped onto one of the guys. This greatly facilitates jibing when the occasion arrives (of which more later).

After the sail is all hooked up as above, keep it and the pole either in the cockpit or on the forward deck in a neat pile and, if approaching a mark up wind, never begin to hoist until after rounding. Hoisting earlier produces harmful windage from the sail and the man setting it. It also invites fouling the sail. If reaching for a mark prior to jibing onto a broader reach or run on the other tack when the spinnaker will be used, don't hoist before the turn has been made. Doing so will only make the jibe more difficult and the sail may foul. When making an off wind start or rounding a mark from a close reach to a broader reach *on the same tack*, the spinnaker may be hoisted beforehand, but it should not be broken until after the boat is settled down on the new course. Saving seconds in getting the spinnaker up and drawing is important; it is less important than being sure that it goes up without a hitch and without interfering with the sailing of the boat.

Before the sail is hoisted, it is well to cleat the end of the sheets and guys. Then, if the spinnaker breaks out prematurely, it won't get out of hand. Be sure to lead the sheet outside the headstay and shrouds, except when using a flat single cut spinnaker.

When hoisting, try to keep too much weight off the bow. One man forward is enough on boats of the size we are considering (under 35 feet over all). The man doing the hoisting should move aft as far as he can and still handle the halliard properly. This maintains the boat's trim. It is well to hoist the spinnaker before lowering the jib. On a run, the helmsman should steer high of the course while the sail is being set, keeping the jib full and drawing and squaring away on the course only after the spinnaker has been broken. Most skippers prefer to break out the spinnaker before lowering the jib. In any event, it is vital to douse the jib promptly in order to get the chute drawing. On a spinnaker reach in fresh air both jib and spinnaker can draw effectively, but on a run or a light air reach the jib should always be lowered.

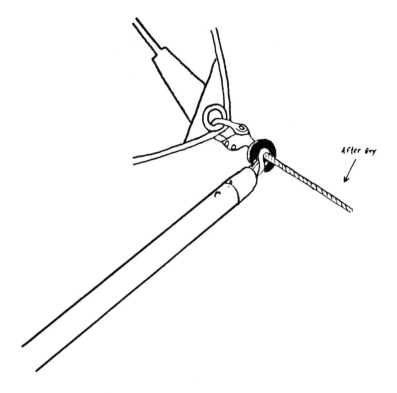

Fig. 45—Note that the after guy is attached to the sail. This permits detaching the pole and still having hold of the sail, and it facilitates jibing since the after guy, which becomes the sheet upon completion of the jibe, is already in place. If the grommets will not accommodate the snap shackles, seize rings onto the clews of the spinnaker and attach the sheet and guy to them.

Note that the pole is attached to the guy just back of a "hockey puck" which prevents it from jamming on the snap shackle splice. To release the spinnaker when dousing it the snap shackle is opened. Should it jam and be unable to open, the sail can be taken in by letting the after guy run free. That's also useful in a knockdown to allow the spinnaker to spill wind.

Avoid Commotion

All sail handling should be done with a minimum of commotion. A well trained crew needs few commands. It learns, also, to work smoothly and fast without much moving about. Especially in light airs, it is essential to stay quiet to keep the boat from rolling and pitching. Failure to do this is sure to shake the wind from the sails and the constant change in trim slows the boat even further.

Once a spinnaker is broken out, it is of utmost importance to keep it properly trimmed. When set, it becomes the most important sail on the boat.

Position of the Pole

The pole should be guyed aft to be not quite at right angles to the *apparent* wind. Apparent wind differs in direction from true wind because of the boat's movement. It comes always further forward than the true wind except on a dead run, when it is the same. The masthead wind pennant shows the direction of apparent wind. The common error is to guy the pole too far aft. If the pole is at right angles to the wind, the tack will be much farther aft than the clew, and wind will spill out of the clew side of the spinnaker. For this reason, the pole should never be guyed all the way back to the shrouds, unless sailing by the lee. Try letting it forward a few feet and watch the boat speed up. Our experience has indicated that it should seldom be guyed further aft than 60° or 70° from the bow.

The spinnaker pole should be level. If one end is higher than the other, the sail is not held out as far as it could be and its full area is presented less efficiently to the wind. To keep it level, a topping lift is attached at the middle of the pole. This is really a halliard for the pole and is especially useful to prevent it from sagging in light airs. In a strong breeze, the outer end is apt to cock up in the air. In this case, the solution is to move the inner end of the pole higher up the mast, thus permitting the desirable lift in the sail and maintaining a level pole in the process. A sliding fitting on a mast track is the best solution for this. If the outer end still tends to cock up even after the pole has been raised to its limit, the forward guy will keep it from going too far. It is sometimes desirable to have it cocking upward *slightly*, particularly in a strong breeze. At all times, forward guy, after guy and topping lift should be taut to keep the pole from flopping around. Otherwise, the wind may easily be shaken out of the spinnaker.

Sheet Lead

The spinnaker sheet should be led outside of the headstay and lee shrouds unless it is a single-luff type sail. On a reach, lead it as far aft as possible. Unless class rules prevent it (they often do) leading to a snatch block on the main boom gives a fine lead.

Put a Good Man on the Sheet

The correct lead is of slight value unless the sheet is trimmed properly. Put your best man on it. He should slack the sheet out as much as possible. On a reach, this will get the luff curving out ahead and reaching for more air. It also prevents the leech from hooking in and backing the main. On a run, the position of the lead is less important but it is just as necessary to slack the sheet as much as possible so that the sail will flow around the headstay and present its full area to the wind.

The sheet tender must be in a position to watch the luff. As soon as it *begins* to break, a sharp quick trim will keep it full. Except in a very fluky breeze, there is no reason for the spinnaker to collapse but, unless it begins to break slightly at frequent intervals, chances are it is too flat. If it does collapse, the helmsman can help get it full again by bearing off slightly.

Ease the Halliard Sometimes

If your boat has jumper stays, they may interfere with the head of the spinnaker on a reach. If the shape is spoiled by laying across a jumper stay, it may prove advantageous to slack the halliard a foot or two to clear it. In a fresh breeze, the halliard may often be slacked to advantage even on a dead run. This permits the sail to belly out ahead better and, because it is lower, there is less tendency for it to bury the bow.

JIBING THE SPINNAKER

With the modern spinnakers which have an identical leech and luff and by using the dip pole method, jibing is a cinch, provided the necessary steps are taken at the right time and in proper sequence. In fact, the sail need not even break in the process. In small boats the old method of disconnecting the inboard end of the pole from the mast, connecting it to the clew, then disconnecting from the old tack of the sail and finally connecting the other end of the pole to the mast is still satisfactory. In larger boats, however, the dip pole method is both safer and easier because the pole is always attached to the mast. Since it can be used effectively on almost all small boats and because its use should be encouraged, this 1983 edition will describe only this system. The dip jibe was unknown years ago (to me anyway and to everyone I ever sailed with or against). Here's the sequence of a dip pole jibe. Referring to Figs. 46A, 46B and 46C as you read this should clarify the procedure.

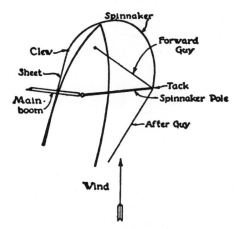

Fig. 46A—The spinnaker set and drawing before the jibe commences.

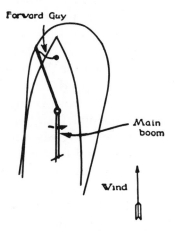

Fig. 46B—The pole has been dipped and is just being attached to the old clew. At this stage the helm is put up and the main boom jibes over.

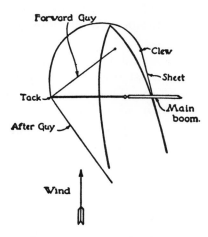

Fig. 46C—With clew un-hooked from the pole, and the pole attached to the mast and squared properly, the jibe is completed.

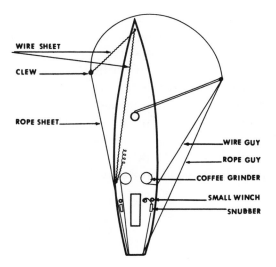

Fig. 46D—This is the rig for the "Vim" jibe, described on page 107.

First slide the inboard end of the pole up to the top of its track or high enough so that when dipped it will swing inside the jibstay.

Then square the pole with the after guy right back to the weather shrouds. If you were on a reach the helmsman must bear off to a run as the pole is squared. As soon as the pole has been squared, lower the topping lift and pull the tripping line at the same instant to release the tack from the pole. If the pole is too long for the crew to reach its outboard end to open the fitting, it should be equipped with a tripping line. *Never* swing the pole forward so you can release the tack. Doing so will bring the spinnaker forward too and it's almost impossible then to keep it full during the jibe.

As the pole is released from the tack and the topping lift is slackened it will swing down and forward between the jibstay and the mast. The spinnaker with the boat now on a dead run will stay full, held only by the guy and sheet.

As the pole swings to the leeward side, pull the sheet in to it and attach the outboard end of the pole either to the sheet (if using the running guy method) or to the ring on the clew. (There's a useful variation on this step which we will present shortly.) While this is being done the main is being trimmed and as soon as the connection has been made the main is jibed over.

Next square the new guy (old sheet), taking up on the outboard end of the pole with the topping lift. Finally lower the inboard end of the pole till it is level at the desired height.

We have not mentioned the forward guy. It remains attached to the outboard end or middle of the pole throughout the evolution. In light air it need not be tended but in a breeze (and especially in large boats) it must be used to keep the pole from flailing about or skying. Once the jibe has been completed and the after guy squared to the desired position, the forward guy must be snugged up immediately.

The evolution described above takes longer to read than to execute. Throughout the helmsman plays a key role. He must time his swing to coincide with the progress of the jibe. The man on the old guy (new sheet) must be sure to trim and the man on the old sheet (new guy) must be sure to ease in order to keep the sail always at right angles to the apparent wind. If all do their job well the sail won't break and the whole evolution is a cinch. If they don't, you know as well as I do the havoc that can take place.

Use of a Jibing Line in the Dip Pole Jibe

There's a refinement on the normal dip pole jibe recommended for all medium sized boats that don't want to go into the complexity of a "Vim" jibe. It consists of the addition of a jibing line (approximately 20′ of ⅜″ dacron for a 40′ boat) with a snaphook on one end. Prior to the jibe this line is snapped into the clew of the spinnaker. When ready to jibe one man goes forward and takes the strain off the sheet by wrapping several turns of this line around a leeward shroud. The sheet is then eased and as the pole is swung across in the jibe it is easy to attach it to this slack sheet. Once attached, the sheet which has now become the guy is trimmed and the jibing line eased. In very heavy air the jibing line should be attached to a mast winch instead of a shroud. Use of a jibing line makes it far easier to connect the pole to the new guy and permits the spinnaker to float high, wide and handsome throughout the evolution. In fact, it has many of the advantages of the Vim jibe, next to be described, without its complexities, and is recommended particularly in boats in the 30' to 50' range.

The "Vim" Jibe

There's a refinement on the jibe described above called the "Vim" jibe after the American Twelve Meter which first developed it. This jibe is useful only on large boats which have wire guys. See Fig. 46D. To execute it is necessary to have both a wire and a rope sheet and guy, one of each led to both the tack and clew of the spinnaker. The wire guy is led from a point a number of feet forward of the rope guy (adjacent to the forward end of the cockpit in a Twelve). The rope guy is led all the way back to the quarter. The strain is taken wholly on the wire and there is just enough tension on the rope guy to keep it clear of the water. So much for the windward side.

On the leeward side all of the tension is taken on the rope which is of course the sheet. A bight in the wire on the leeward side is taken forward to the jibstay.

The jibe is done in the same manner as in a normal dip pole jibe but with these variations: As the wire guy is squared take up also on the rope guy to get it reasonably taut.

As the pole swings through between the jibstay and the mast, snap the bight of the wire sheet into it. This can be done very rapidly as the pole swishes by. As soon as the connection has been made the main boom is swung over and the old wire sheet is trimmed rapidly on the coffee grinder. It does, of course, become the guy. While it is being trimmed the rope guy (ex-rope sheet) controls the tack of the spinnaker. It is trimmed to a second winch, smaller than the coffee grinder but powerful enough to do the job while the boat is on a run. When the wire has been trimmed enough to get the tack out to the end of the pole it then takes the strain and the rope guy can be eased.

On the other side (which had been the windward side and after jibing becomes the leeward side) the strain is then taken on the wire sheet (ex-wire guy) and the spinnaker is at first controlled by it. The rope sheet, however, is then trimmed taut on a small winch or by hand, then held at the proper trim by a snubber. At this point, the wire sheet is cast off the coffee grinder winch drum and the rope sheet put onto it. The snubber is then released. A bight of the wire sheet is then led forward to be ready for the next jibe.

Advantages of the "Vim" jibe are that the hookup can be made instantly as the pole swishes by, without having to pull the old sheet or old clew over to the pole end. This would take time, disturb the shape of the spinnaker and also, on a large boat, be very difficult. By attaching to a guy which has no strain on it and which at the time is led to where it can readily be attached, it all becomes easy. Moreover the sail can be kept in perfect control throughout the maneuver.

This method is not recommended on small boats because it requires too many in crew to handle the double sheets and guys and also requires extra fittings. On large boats, however, it is now a must as a crew's brawn is no match for the forces exerted and the smaller boat method simply can't do it as fast. An America's Cup crew, using this method, can complete a jibe in 10 seconds in a 25 knot wind, without the chute ever breaking. Five seconds later (just enough time to get the wire bight forward on the leeward side) they are all set to jibe back again. Jibing duels with crews such as these can be carried out more rapidly than tacking duels. In fact, much the hardest job, if it's blowing, is to get the main over.

TAKING IN THE SPINNAKER

Little difficulty need be experienced when it comes to taking in the spinnaker, providing proper procedure is used.

The first step is to have the halliard clear for running, and to make sure that the sheets and guys are also clear. Then, if the race is still in progress, hoist the jib and trim and clear it for the course which will be sailed after the spinnaker has been doused.

At this point, the foredeck man takes his station, the helmsman runs off a bit before the wind *if there is room to do so* and only if there is a strong wind (running before it lessens the strength of the apparent wind and facilitates spinnaker handling). One crew member slacks the after guy while another tends the sheet. The guy is then either detached from the spinnaker tack or allowed to run free. The sail flies ahead and to leeward, held only by the sheet, and the halliard. The man formerly tending the after guy now takes charge of the halliard. Meanwhile the sheet has been trimmed quickly and the foot of the sail gathered in to leeward of the main and clear of the spreaders. The halliard is lowered and the sail pulled down into the cockpit. The whole evolution takes 10 to 15 seconds *or less*.

It is important to keep the sail clear of the spreaders and, when lowering, to make sure that it does not get in the water. If it does get overboard, be sure not to let it act as a scoop. Hold only one end, never both tack and clew, and it should then be a relatively simple matter to bring it back on board.

A recent innovation is a retrieving line attached approximately to the middle of the spinnaker. With sails so equipped, dousing is a bit different as well as a bit faster. When it comes time to douse, one or more crew members grab the retrieving line, which has been led under the jib. Then the halliard is lowered smartly and the retrieving line pulled in rapidly. The negative of this method is the fact that the spinnaker always has a retrieving line attached to it, which can impair its ability to lift in light air. There is also the possibility of this line fouling on the rigging. But it does make for superfast douses, enabling the crew to carry the spinnaker right up to the leeward mark, which can be useful either in breaking or maintaining an overlap.

SMALL BOAT SPINNAKER TECHNIQUE

The heading of this section is in some respects a misnomer because this method is becoming increasingly popular on boats 50 feet and larger, particularly the system of setting flying (but not so much the running guy which isn't necessary on larger boats). In the case of large boats, however, a bag or turtle is substituted for the box or launching bin or tube hereafter mentioned, with the spinnaker being flaked into it with clews and head protruding. A short length of line or a stop should be sewn to the bottom of the bag to permit lashing to a padeye or life line stanchion on deck.

The method, however, is especially suitable for small boats and hence the name. The key to its success, in addition to setting flying, is to snap the outboard end of the pole, not to the spinnaker tack or after guy fitting, but instead to the running part of the guy. Fig. 46E illustrates the proper sort of setup.

With the arrangement, the pole can be rigged on the mast prior to reaching the mark, and when at the mark the spinnaker hoisted in the protected lee of the mainsail and then pulled around the jibstay to the pole end. In boats such as Lightnings, where the method has come into most favor, the whole evolution can be completed without anyone ever leaving the cockpit.

To make sure we've got this simple and effective method down pat, it might be helpful if we considered it step by step.

Prior to the start, try to decide which tack the spinnaker will be first set on. Then lead the after guy through a quarter block, outside the shrouds, around the jibstay and to what will become the lee shrouds. The sheet is then led through a quarter block, outside the lee shrouds and its end snapped to the

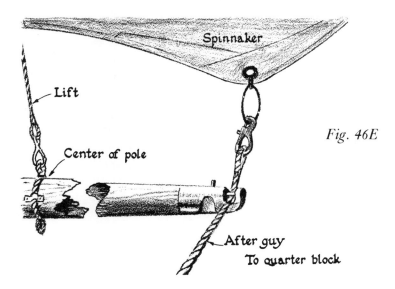

Fig. 46E

end of the after guy. If you later discover that the spinnaker leg will be on the other tack, merely pull the guy and sheet around the bow so that their ends are adjacent to the chainplates on the other side.

Next place your spinnaker in a box. We use a cardboard beer carton and carry a spare under our forward deck in case one goes overboard. In boxing the spinnaker, first take one clew and place it in one corner of the box. We keep it in place by slitting the corner about one-third of its height. Then run your hand along the foot and slip the other clew into the slit in the adjacent corner of the box (see detail, Fig. 46F).

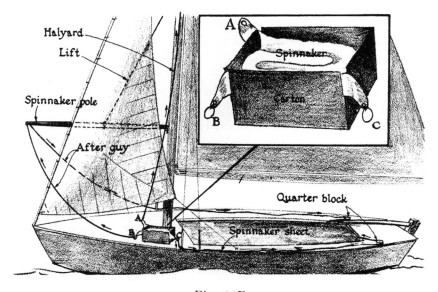

Fig. 46F

Next run your hand up the two leeches simultaneously, flaking them into the box and stuffing the body of the sail in at the same time. This running along the foot and luffs insures against twists. When you've reached the head, slip it into the slit in a third corner of the box. The spinnaker can now be put away until ready for use.

When nearing the weather mark, one crew member takes out the pole, clips its end onto the running part of the after guy, attaches the lift and then sets the other end in the mast fitting. If the downwind leg is to be on the same tack as that on which the mark is approached the pole lays against the jibstay. (See Fig. 46F). If on the other hand, one has to tack around the mark or jibe immediately after rounding, the pole can still be rigged ahead of time on most boats with no overlapping jibs. On a Lightning, for example, there's just room for the rigged pole to pass between the lee shrouds and the leech of the jib. (See Fig. 46G). In this position, it extends off to leeward and care must be taken to give the mark and right-of-way yachts on that side an adequate berth.

With the pole rigged on the windward side, and also before reaching the mark, the spinnaker box is taken out from its shelter, the guy is attached to the tack, the sheet to the clew and finally the halliard. In light and moderate going, the box can be placed on deck, to leeward of the jib.

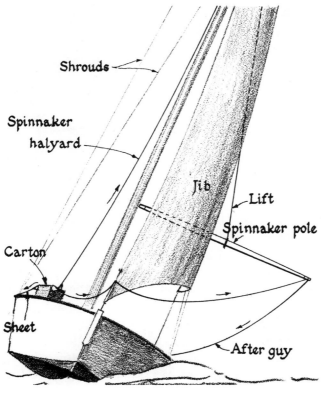

Fig. 46G

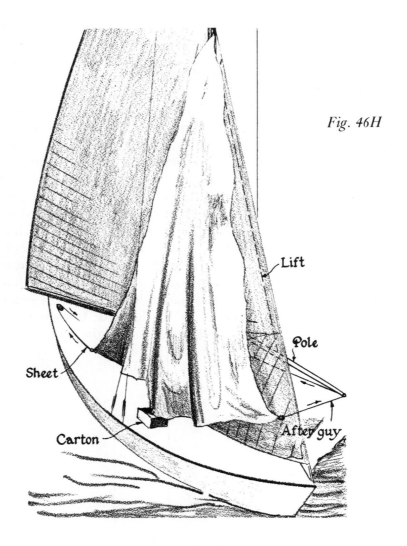

Fig. 46H

Lift

Pole

Sheet

Carton

After guy

This makes it easier to be sure that it will hoist clear and to leeward of the main and jib. On some boats there is room on deck to place the box inboard of the lee shrouds to keep it from sliding overboard. In heavy going it is often better to keep the box in the cockpit. The sheet, guy and halliard can still be attached, taking care to lead them so that they will run clear when hoisting. Be sure not to lead them between the jib sheet and the deck, but over the jib sheet.

If the pole is rigged to leeward prior to tacking around the mark or in anticipation of jibing after rounding, the box is on the windward deck and sheet, guy and halliard are attached as shown in Fig. 46G.

Now that you'r'e rigged, anyone can set spinnaker. (See Fig. 46H). Assume we have a three-man crew, skipper and two others. As soon as the mark is reached on the tack you will be running on, or as soon as jibe is completed, one man hoists spinnaker as fast as possible and belays when within half a foot or so of "two-blocks." As soon as it is up and while it is still being belayed, the other crew who has been checking that the sail ran up clear from the box, tosses the empty box back in the cockpit and hauls on the after guy to pull the tack up to the pole end. While this is being done and while using one hand to belay the halliard, the No. 1 crew man uses his other hand to hold the pole forward against the jibstay. Were he not to do this, the pole would swing aft as the guy was trimmed, and this would make it slow and difficult to pull the spinnaker around the jib. If the leg was a reach it would also make the spinnaker back as soon as it cleared the jib.

At this point when the tack reaches the pole end, the No. 1 crew man either relieves the No. 2 crew of the after guy or he grabs the spinnaker sheet. We find it better for the No. 1 crew to take the guy, trim it to approximately the right spot and belay. He then lowers jib, while the No. 2 crew is handling the spinnaker sheet.

We've omitted the skipper's role but suffice it to say that in addition to handling the main sheet the skipper can frequently lend a hand on the spinnaker sheet or guy, to speed the process of setting. Constant practice will enable a three-man crew to work smoothly and complete the whole operation in a few seconds.

No mention has been made of a forward guy, for the simple reason that on many small boats such as Lightnings, one is unnecessary. Many such boats have a hook attached to the deck adjacent to the shrouds. By leading the after guy under this hook, there is enough downward pull to make a forward guy unnecessary. We have found that it is better not to lead the guy under this hook until the spinnaker is squared. Leading under the hook prior to this just slows up the process of pulling the sail out to the pole end.

If you must have a forward guy, connect it to the middle of the pole beneath the lift. (See Fig. 46E). If in strong winds this results in the pole bending up excessively on a reach, snap the forward guy onto the end of the pole. If at all possible on your boat, however, try doing without a forward guy. It's a great convenience not to have this additional line to handle.

With this method of spinnaker setting and rigging the evolution of jibing is handled in the conventional manner, with the exception that when the pole is shifted over the new outboard end is snapped onto the running part of the guy, just as it was on the other tack. This is important, because the new method has its advantages while dousing spinnaker as well as while setting.

In taking in the spinnaker it is not necessary to leave the cockpit of a small boat. Make sure the after guy is coiled down, has no knot in it and is ready to run clear. Then, when ready to take in spinnaker, let the pole forward and then let the after guy run free. It will shoot through the pole end and the crew man on the sheet can pull the sail in to leeward of the main in the usual manner. The big advantage, of course, is that no one has to go on the foredeck to unsnap the tack. How many centerboarders have capsized because of forward weight!

One might expect that the guy would occasionally fail to run clear, but in several seasons' use ours never has.

I've been asked if I preferred this method to a turtle. The answer is yes. In the first place, boats with their jibstays right up to the stem cannot use a turtle. Even in boats which can use a turtle, this box method seems just as fast, though no faster. It has a real advantage if the spinnaker is to be reset because the crew can much more easily rearrange the spinnaker into a box than into a turtle lashed on the stem, and can do so, moreover, without slowing the boat down by standing on the bow.

One note of caution: One must be careful that the slack after guy doesn't fall under the bow. If it does, one could pull the spinnaker under the boat as it is hoisted, or be unable to pull it around. This happened to us once; now we keep our eyes peeled to see that it doesn't again. Some Lightning skippers guard against this by lashing a projection forward of the stem. A wire coat-hanger bent into the form of a 6" bowsprit is effective and insures against the guy slipping down the stem. Before rigging this, however, be sure your class rules don't outlaw such a gadget.

To sum up, I've a suspicion that once you've tried this method of spinnaker setting and dousing you will never switch away from it. We approached it with some skepticism but we're now sold on it.

In describing this method of spinnaker setting I have referred to the use of a box, in which the sail is stowed prior to hoisting. Nowadays many boats have bins which serve the same purpose. If yours does, use the bin, not the box, and connect in the same way.

Still other boats have tubes underneath the foredecks with an opening forward of the jibstay. The chute is stuffed into the tube with sheet, guy, and halliard attached to the clews and head. To set, all you have to do is hoist smartly and then trim the sheet and the guy (which has been led through the pole's end), and an almost instantaneous set is accomplished. When it comes time to douse, the spinnaker is sucked back into the tube, with sheet and guy still attached, ready to be reset whenever required.

If your boat is equipped with a tube launcher or a bin, by all means use it. If not, setting from a box or turtle, or on a larger boat from a bag or box, is the way to go.

With a good crew it's possible to stay in control on a run in a very strong breeze. This J-24 is going so fast that the apparent wind strength is reduced.

International No. 25 in the safe leeward position has a perfect start. The lower photo, a few seconds later, shows how she has backwinded No. 22 and forged ahead.

The leeward end is favored and the boats near the committee boat are already far behind. But the bold mid-line starters are in good shape.

You've got to risk a wipe-out if you hope to win in keen company.

How not to carry a spinnaker; the wind is too far ahead and the pole cocked up too high. The sail buries the boat instead of increasing her speed.

CHRISTOPHER CUNNINGHAM

Catamarans are now recognized as the fastest boats afloat. This Boston Whaler Super-Cat is going faster than the apparent wind. Board boats, too, have blazing speed, and their popularity is increasing rapidly.

WINDSURFING INTERNATIONAL, INC.

Flying Dutchman 83 took a chance and got away with it. FD 184 left the mark just wide enough for FD 83 to sneak inside.

MORRIS ROSENFELD

In the top picture, International No. 17 has the choice spot at the mark. No. 20 is in a tough spot. No. 15, provided she can find a hole, may pass several boats.

DIANE BEESTON

When approaching the weather mark in a big fleet it pays to be on starboard. G6291 is losing a number of positions and is in danger of fouling.

Many modern boats have spinnaker launchers to simplify things *(top)*. But then they also have a lot of strings attached, as shown by this modern Finn *(below)*.

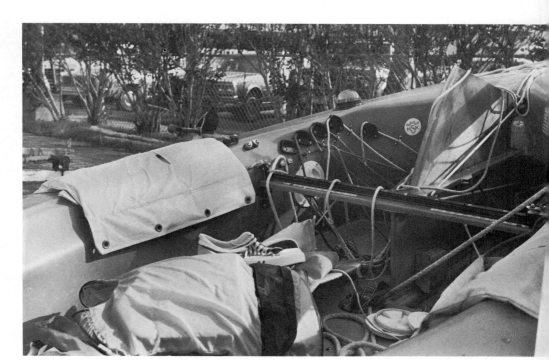

Careful trim keeps Buddy Melges's Soling
on her feet in this hard blow.

Sometimes discretion is in order. I'll bet *Hotpants* didn't set her spinnaker.

In a singlehander like this Laser even teeth come in handy.

The Star class is over seventy years old, but has remained
modern by adopting modern technology. Buddy Melges in action.

PETER BARLOW

Collision at the first mark *(top)*. Peter Barlow reports that a second after he took this photo the impact sounded like someone stepping on a box of shredded wheat. If crossing on port tack, do it by a safe margin. In the bottom photo *Fox* cleared more easily than this telephoto lens shot might indicate.

MITCH CARUCCI

By heeling to windward on a run the sailor aboard Sunfish 908 has neutralized helm and maximized rig efficiency.

When reaching in tight quarters like this, take care to give a boat to leeward a sufficient berth so that your spinnaker doesn't brush her weather shroud.

More fouls occur and more distance is gained or lost at jibe marks than at any other time in a race. No fouls here yet, but *Zuma* and 1062 will both drop back by being outside, and a foul between them could occur.

With current like this it is certain trouble if you haven't given the mark a wide berth. Take constant bearings as you approach, and if they are slipping, tack away in time.

PETER BARLOW

A sudden release of the spinnaker sheet by the boat to windward could have saved her from this wild broach, with the loss of maybe half a length instead of five or more.

X

Rounding Marks

ROUNDING THE MARK ranks second only to the start as the most important single moment of the average race. Only after you have seen boats sailing almost even for an entire leg and then suddenly become well spread out following the eventful moments of the turn, and only after you yourself have lost three or four places in such a situation, can the need for skill at this time be appreciated.

The Importance of the Approach

When approaching the lee mark, especially if the fleet is large and well bunched, it is well to try to get the inside position at the turn. If you fail to do this, and some boat at the last minute gains an overlap, more than this one position may be lost. If the next leg is to windward, after rounding, you are in danger of being blanketed by the boat which slipped inside, and then others that rounded just astern, being already on your quarter, might pass also. Furthermore, by being down to leeward as a result of the wide turn, you may be unable to tack and clear your wind because of the proximity of the boats on your weather quarter. Of course, when the next leg is a reach or a run, the initial loss by being outside is equally great but is less apt to be prolonged and accentuated, since, by reaching up or off, a clear wind may be obtained.

Gaining the Inside Position

There are several ways by which the inside position may be gained, but all of them involve planning well ahead. Frequently, as early as the start, it is advisable to plan to cross on the end of the line which will ultimately give the inside at the turn. Assuming, however, that one-quarter mile from the mark your boat is well outside the bulk of the fleet, it is then usually advisable (especially if the fleet is large and close enough to profit if you make a poor

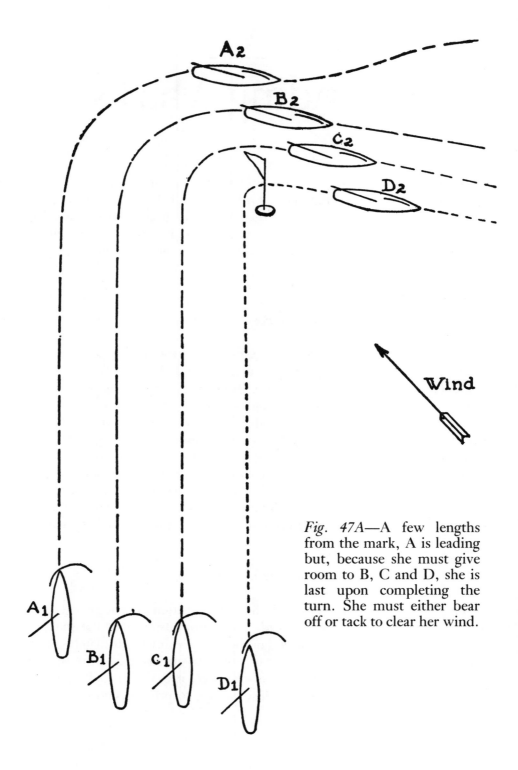

Fig. 47A—A few lengths from the mark, A is leading but, because she must give room to B, C and D, she is last upon completing the turn. She must either bear off or tack to clear her wind.

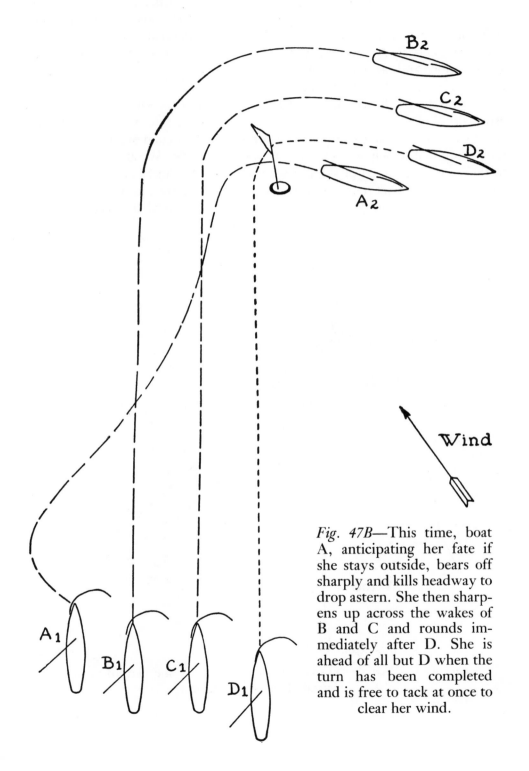

Wind

Fig. 47B—This time, boat A, anticipating her fate if she stays outside, bears off sharply and kills headway to drop astern. She then sharpens up across the wakes of B and C and rounds immediately after D. She is ahead of all but D when the turn has been completed and is free to tack at once to clear her wind.

turn) to bear off or reach up, as the case may be, to get the inside berth. In so
doing, it may be necessary to kill way and go under the stern of several boats
that you otherwise had a slim chance of beating to the mark but, even so, this
is the safer course. An overlap at the last minute may enable you to regain the
lost positions and, at worst, you will have sacrificed fewer places than if you
had rounded outside. (Fig. 47A and 47B).

At this point, however, a word of caution is necessary. Many sailors,
especially those who have just been caught on the outside, resolve that never
again will they be outside and never again will a boat get an overlap on them if
they can possibly help it. In their zeal, they go too far. We are here referring
to that annoying breed of skipper who would rather luff half a mile off the
course than let a boat remain close on his weather quarter, in striking distance
of an overlap. If you don't wish to be sailed right out of the race, the only

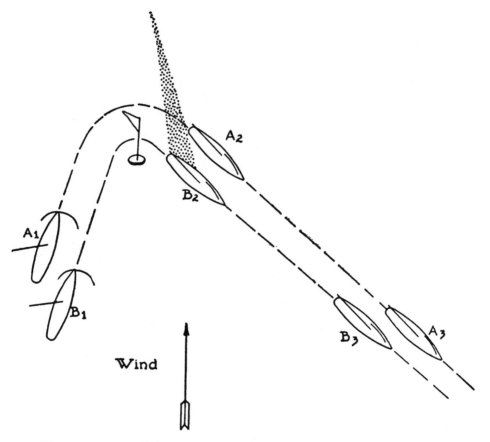

Fig. 48A—Boat A rounds as close under B as she can and gains
the safe leeward position.

thing to do is kill way enough to be able to bear off under his stern. Then you can sit back as the mark approaches and enjoy the spectacle of the offender getting the medicine he so richly deserves. All the boats to leeward, and many astern, will almost invariably slip through his lee if he has gone too far to windward. They are approaching the mark closer on the wind and, therefore, sail much faster than a boat far to windward and squared away to get down to the mark. It really doesn't do a great deal of good to get the inside turn if there are no boats to be inside of left in your class.

Defense Against an Overlap

If you are unable to get the inside berth at the mark, and another boat gains an overlap, all is not lost. Especially if the next leg is to windward and, providing the overlap is not excessive, it may be possible to shake her off. But

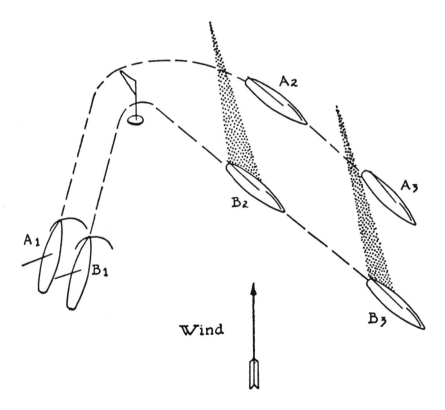

Fig. 48B—Boat B has too great an overlap for A to gain the safe leeward position. A's best chance is to bear off after rounding to keep her wind clear. If she is faster than B she will be able to draw ahead.

only if you make a good turn. If the other boat has only a slight overlap, your best chance lies in giving her just enough room and rounding as close to her as possible. You may then be able to gain the safe leeward position as indicated in Fig. 48A and your opponent will either drop astern or be forced to tack to clear her wind.

If your competitor's overlap is greater, such tactics may result in getting yourself blanketed. In this case, your best chance lies in making a wide turn and reaching off a bit after rounding. (Fig. 48B). By so doing, you will be able to maintain a clear wind and then, if your boat is faster, either outfoot the other boat or work up under her later on and assume the safe leeward position. In any event, an overlap need not be fatal to the outside boat unless the inside one is ahead as the turn commences. Then your best bet is to give her only enough room to pass inside and plan to tack to clear your wind as soon as possible.

Overlaps will always be fatal to the outside boat unless she executes the turn properly. In Figs. 48A and 48B, we noted how the outside boat should round. Fig. 48C shows how *not* to do it. The outside boat leaves too wide a berth at first, then rounds up too soon. Her only chance is to tack at once.

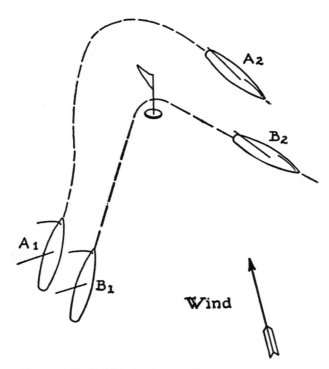

Fig. 48C—Boat A shows how not to round a
mark. She ends up being blanketed by B.

Rounding Alone

Suppose, however, that you are approaching a lee mark without having to worry about giving room. The manner in which the turn is made is still important. Several rules should be obeyed. First of all, don't swing so fast that you will lose headway. Second, make sure that neither tide nor sea causes you to hit the buoy but, on the other hand, don't be afraid to cut it close. The skipper who has reckoned with all conditions can safely pass it close aboard. If the next leg is to windward, it is desirable to give the mark a good berth to one side at the beginning of the swing, so that at the conclusion you will cut it close, and be as far to windward as possible. If you cut it close on the reaching course, before coming on to the wind, you will be a length farther to leeward than necessary. This is not a loss in distance because you got there a length sooner but it can cause a loss if the following boat rounds correctly and, by being close to your weather quarter, makes tacking impossible. (Fig. 49).

Jibing Around the Mark

In jibing around the mark from one spinnaker reach to another, the skipper, by the course he steers, can facilitate jibing the parachute. A gradual turn is desirable. By going a bit to windward just before getting to the mark, and then squaring off dead before the wind for the couple of lengths immediately prior to reaching the buoy, the crew has time to get the spinnaker shifted for the next reach, so that as soon as the turn is made it fills and is ready to draw. The slight distance lost in this kind of approach is more than offset by the resulting fast and neat jibe, which all but removes the danger of twisting the spinnaker around the headstay and enables it to draw sooner.

Approaching the Weather Mark

Turning to a consideration of the weather mark, it is immediately obvious that here the approach is of the utmost importance. If possible, it is well to plan your course to arrive at the mark on the starboard tack. Assume that the mark must be left to starboard, so that if approaching on the starboard tack it will be necessary to go about to round it. If a bunch of boats is approaching on the port tack at the same time, they will be forced to go about until the starboard tack boat has swung to round. This is an obvious advantage for the right-of-way boat. If this advantage is to be realized, however, it is imperative for the starboard tack boat to be approaching the mark close aboard. If she can

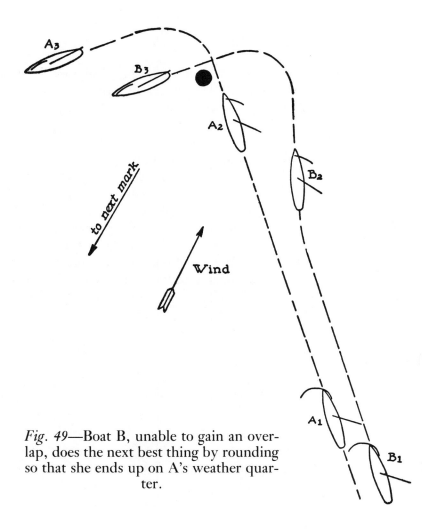

Fig. 49—Boat B, unable to gain an overlap, does the next best thing by rounding
so that she ends up on A's weather quarter.

fetch only within fifty yards or so of the mark, her advantages have, to a great
extent, disappeared. In this case, if the port tack boats are laying the mark
right on the nose, they can fake going about and, at the last minute, bear off
under the stern of the boat on the starboard tack. Then, by pinching a trifle,
they can still fetch and stand a good chance of rounding first. (Fig. 50). If the
starboard tack boat had tried to avoid this by tacking on the other boat's lee
bow she might then have been unable to fetch. In either case, her starboard
tack advantage has disappeared. If approaching the mark close aboard, however, there would be no room for the other boats to pass under her stern and
still be able to round the mark. (Fig. 51).

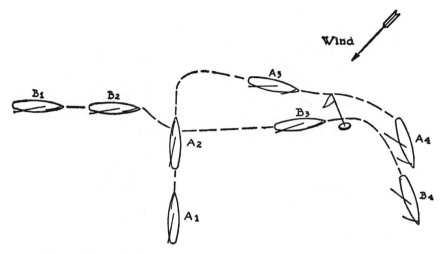

Fig. 50—Boat B bears off under A's stern and rounds first. Had A been approaching the mark close abroad, this would have been impossible.

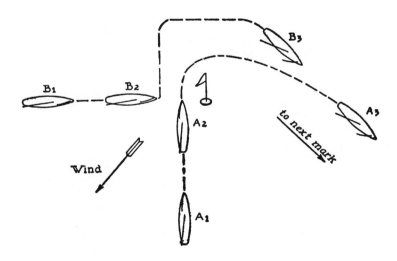

Fig. 51—Boat B has no room to pass under A's stern and still round the mark. She must tack and A rounds first.

The importance of arriving at the weather mark on the starboard tack must be remembered while still some distance from the mark, and tactics governed accordingly. Imagine yourself 200 yards dead to leeward of the mark, on the port tack, and converging with a boat on the starboard tack. You are a few feet ahead, but not far enough to cross her bow. Some skippers in this situation might want impulsively to tack on the other boat's lee bow to get a safe leeward position. Such tactics should never be practiced while close to the mark. Though the safe leeward position would, in the long run, permit you to work out a lead, it may be impossible in the short remaining distance to sail clear ahead. If this happened, and you were not far enough ahead to tack across your competitor's bow, he could hold you on the starboard tack until he could easily lay the mark, by which time you would have overstood. When he does tack, though you follow suit immediately, he will have gotten the jump and will probably round first. (Fig. 52A).

To have avoided all this would have been simple. When converging with the starboard tack boat, instead of tacking on her lee bow, the better course

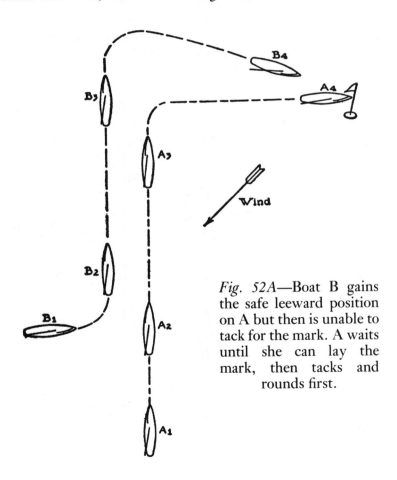

Fig. 52A—Boat B gains the safe leeward position on A but then is unable to tack for the mark. A waits until she can lay the mark, then tacks and rounds first.

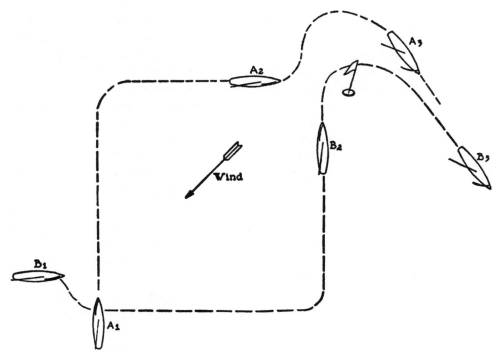

Fig. 52B—Had B borne off under A, as shown here, she would stand a good chance of forcing A about at the mark and rounding first.

would have been to bear off just under her stern and swing onto the starboard tack only when the mark can be approached close aboard. Such tactics will permit approaching the mark on the starboard tack, thus protecting you from all the other boats in the fleet and, unless the boat which has just crossed you has traveled faster than you have, will enable you to round ahead of her. (Fig. 52B). If both boats have traveled at the same speed, it would be too dangerous for your competitor to attempt to cross your bow, since the clearance would be only a matter of inches at the most, and it is unlikely that, in the short time afforded, she could hope to open up a safe margin.

Even when approaching virtually alone, there are certain mistakes to be avoided. The most common of these is overstanding. Every length sailed after you could *safely* lay the mark is a length thrown away, and this distance may be the ultimate difference between victory and defeat. A more serious loss, however, often results from not going far enough. This necessitates two extra tacks at the last minute and results in a loss of headway and several boat lengths of distance. It is well to continue a length or two beyond the position when you first think you can lay the mark, because this extra distance can be partially made up by easing sheets and traveling faster after tacking, when it is certain that the mark can be fetched. Overstanding a length or two is not an error but a precaution. On the other hand, when a skipper habitually goes six or seven boat lengths too far, he should do something about it. While out for a sail and before and after races he might practice estimating when he can lay a mark and then tack for it to see how close he comes to being right. Determine how high your boat can point and learn to sight across the cockpit at a certain position, or across the after part of the cabin, in the direction she will fetch on the opposite tack. Some skippers even paint lines on their decks which head in the direction their boat can point on the opposite tack. But remember that in light airs or in a heavy sea she will be unable to point as high as in fresh winds and smooth waters. Remember also that, under certain conditions, the tide will set her to leeward and in others it will enable her to fetch a mark more easily than might have been expected. But, above all, remember that practice makes perfect and with practice you should be able to make accurate estimates of when you can tack safely to lay a mark.

The weather mark may be passed close without fear of fouling since there is no spinnaker still aloft, or on the way down, which might be blown to leeward and inadvertently foul the buoy.

Once safely around a mark, either windward or leeward, there is no greater satisfaction than to look back and see a jam of boats killing each other's way, and to realize that proper tactics alone prevented your own boat from being involved. That is, there is no greater satisfaction unless (as is often the case) this slight jump stretches into a permanent lead and you cross the line a winner.

XI

Playing the Current

Racing without a knowledge of current is like walking up an escalator that is going down. Lake water sailors need not consider tidal effects but those who race on salt water and rivers must do so if they hope to win consistently. Current is of far greater strength, and hence of more importance, in some areas than in others, but in all coastal waters it plays some part.

Strictly speaking, tide is the vertical rise and fall of water, but it is attended by a current, most noticeable in long narrow bays, which moves in a horizontal direction. Tidal current is often referred to as tide, and hence we will use the terms interchangeably.

Tide has little effect on a boat's passage *through* the water. Instead, the whole body of water moves and the boat, which is sailing therein, is carried along with it. Consequently, her speed over the bottom is changed and that's what counts. The primary object of a skipper who is racing in a tideway is to get in the location of strongest current when it is going his way and into the weakest tide when it is running against him.

It should be remembered throughout the following discussion, however, that tide is only one aspect of the race and that there are other conditions which dictate which is the best course. In some cases, the tide is the biggest factor and the course should be governed almost entirely by the effort to stay in the location of most favorable (or least unfavorable) current. At other times, wind, sea or the position of competitors may be considerations of far greater importance. In the latter instances, it might be best to select a course in which the tide is known to be unfavorable. At all times, whether utilized, or disregarded because wind is the dominant factor, tide and its effect should be reckoned with before choosing one's course. It should then be used to a greater or lesser extent, or not at all, as the skipper's judgment indicates. In order to decide intelligently, a knowledge of general and local tidal characteristics is essential.

General Tidal Characteristics

While tide acts differently in various locations, it possesses certain general characteristics. It seldom runs as strong close to shore as it does farther out. In Long Island Sound, for example, the tide is strongest in the center and a bit weaker on both shores. This is similar to the current in a river which flows less swiftly along the banks than in the middle. From the above it may be concluded that to gain the chief benefit of a favoring tide one should sail a mile or so off the shore, and when bucking the tide it is best to hug one shore or another. The above rules apply to most areas.

Tide is usually strongest in deep water and much valuable information can be gleaned by watching the charts and staying in shallow water when avoiding it. This is not always the case, since hard and rocky bottom may not

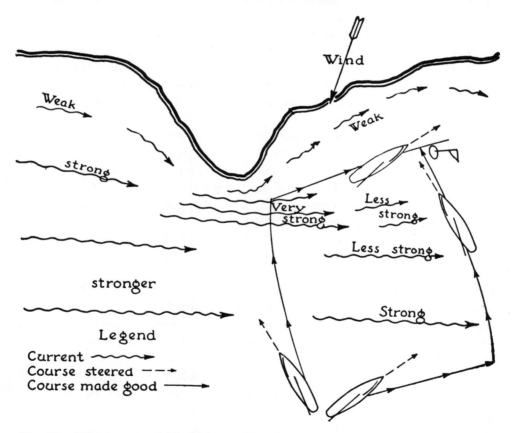

Fig. 53—The boat at the left, by tacking inshore directly off the point, stays in a stronger fair tide and reaches the mark first.

scour away as easily as softer bottom and the tide over such bottom may actually be stronger than in nearby places where water is deeper. The charts give all this information and intelligent study usually gives a clue to the place where tides are less. One can tell the strength of tide and direction by watching for choppy water. Flotsam usually indicates a back eddy. Short choppy waves indicate tide against the wind.

Another characteristic which may be relied on is that tide is strongest off points, and in this case close to shore. If the water is shoal off a point, this may not be true, but otherwise it may be relied on. This characteristic can be utilized to great advantage. If beating to windward in a favoring tide, it is helpful to take a tack which heads toward a point and keeps you in line with it for a longer time. If you sail parallel to the shore line past the point, the stronger tide would be passed sooner and then, upon tacking inshore later on, there would be less tide under you. (Fig. 53).

Beyond and behind a point, the tide is weaker and becomes increasingly so as one nears the shore. The point acts as a barrier to its advance and slows it down. Very close to the shore, sometimes it even forms a back eddy and travels in the opposite direction from the main body of the tide. (Fig. 54). The advantage of reaching this back eddy when bucking a tide is obvious. It is often worth sailing well off the course to get into when the tide is foul. Conversely, this area should be avoided when the tide is with you. Even if there is no back eddy, the tide is generally weaker in indentations of the

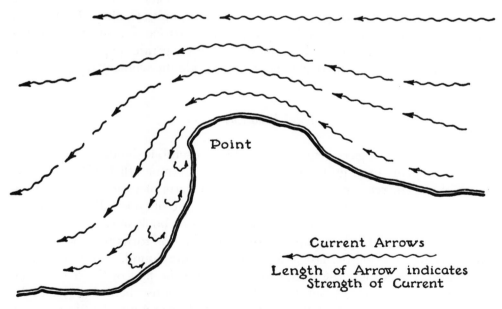

Point

Current Arrows

Length of Arrow indicates
Strength of Current

Fig. 54—Note the way a point affects the direction and velocity of the tide.

shoreline and in bays. Also, it is weaker along a curving shore than a straight one, and this fact may be used to advantage.

The reader may have noticed in Fig. 54 that tide tends to conform in direction with the shore. It sweeps into and out of bays and inlets, usually at slower speed than the main body of tide moving along in the general direction of the coast. A knowledge of these changes of direction is of obvious advantage.

In narrow entrances to harbors, bays or larger bodies of water, the velocity of tide is greatly increased. The large mass of water from the larger body must pass through the narrow opening. Hence it is forced through at greater speed. In the Gut, a narrow entrance to Long Island Sound, velocity reaches 4.4 knots and in the Race, another narrow entrance, it gets as high as 5.2 knots. The total width of both entrances is about 7 miles; this is so much less than the 17-mile width of the Sound at its widest part that these very high velocities result when the vast amount of water is forced through these narrow entrances. The same principle applies everywhere.

We have already noted that tide flows less rapidly behind points than further off shore. Islands and shoals have a similar effect. Directly behind an island, the current is less than it is on either side. To pass through a narrow opening between a point and an island, one's best chance is to work up behind the island (or the point) rather than buck the full stream of tide which rushes through the opening. (Fig. 55). Boat A sails the best course because she keeps out of the strong tide by sailing in the lee of the island. When crossing the strongest current, she is on a beam reach—a fast point of sailing. Boat C also sails a good course but passes through the area of strong tide on a broad reach and hence travels slower and remains in the strong tide longer. B sails the worst course, because she bucks the strongest tide the whole way.

Local Tidal Conditions

While a knowledge of general tidal habits is useful, it should be augmented by more specific local information. The Hydrographic office of the Department of Commerce publishes Tidal Current Charts of various areas. Every skipper should have one of his area. They may be obtained direct from the Department or from local marine supply stores or book stores. The one for Long Island Sound, for example, shows that the tide turns first close to the shore. When bucking the last of an ebb tide on the Sound, many races have been won by getting close to the shore and into the first of the flood while one's opponents were still out where the tide was against them. It doesn't take much of a tide to make a whale of a difference. A boat with a half knot better tide gains *about 500 feet in ten minutes*. No wonder tide is important!

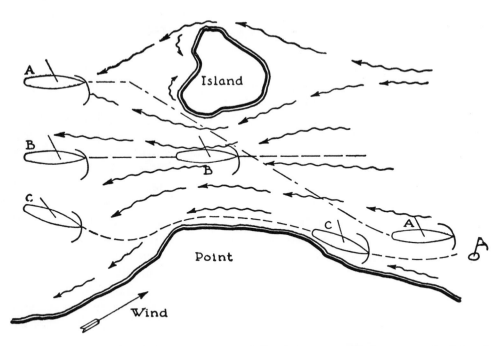

Fig. 55—Boat A combats most successfully the strong tide between the island and the point. Why is her course better than C's?

Personal observation must be added to the information supplied on current charts to provide a well rounded picture of local tidal habits. And remember that conditions will change at various times. The circular tells the time the tide will turn. One knows that it runs for approximately six hours, that it is of diminished velocity for the hour or so before and after slack high and slack low water and runs fastest approximately midway between the time of high and low water. But that isn't the whole story. At the time of full moon, a greater rise and fall of tide occurs and with it an increase in velocity. A very strong wind blowing steadily from one direction will tend to increase the velocity of tide if both are traveling in the same direction and decrease it when the wind is blowing against the tide. Wind will also affect the time the tide turns and its eventual height.

What if Tide Cannot Be Avoided?

Avoiding a foul tide or getting the most out of a fair one are not the only means by which a knowledge of tide is helpful in winning races. There are times when it is impossible to avoid its effects, times when all boats are bound to experience tide of equal strength. Even so, there remain rules for allowing for the tide and for taking advantage of it most successfully.

At the start, when there is a strong tide running, tactics must be governed accordingly. Unless the effect of tide is reckoned with, one will be late at the start in a head tide and over early in a fair one. Timing must be modified to avoid either. Especially in light airs, if there is a head tide, stay near the line or even the wrong side of the line until just before the start. If early, it is simple to kill way to avoid beating the gun. A fair tide presents an even greater problem at the start when the wind is light. If you get over ahead of the gun, it may be many minutes before you can get back and, if the breeze is very light, it may be utterly impossible to return. In the meantime, your competitors will be drifting with the tide in the direction of the first mark and will open up an unbeatable lead. Under such conditions, plan to be a bit late at the line. Play it safe, because otherwise the odds are too heavily against you. Have a light anchor ready, with line bent on. If it appears that you may be swept over early, drop the anchor to stop your headway. Incidentally, an anchor is a valuable asset throughout a light wind race whenever the tide is foul. If the breeze peters out you are apt to be losing ground even though you are still sailing through the water. Under such conditions, check your progress by taking ranges on landmarks. If you see you are losing, drop the anchor over quietly and, if possible, without your competitors seeing it. You may be able to gain quite a lead before they realize they are going backward.

Lee Bowing the Tide

It is quite generally believed that, when beating almost directly against the current, it is helpful to sail a bit higher than usual in order to lee bow the tide. It is argued that so doing will result in the boat being pushed to windward and will enable her to get to the weather mark sooner. In fact, in the earlier editions of this book, I expounded just such a thesis and only two persons ever called me on it. When they did disagree, however, it got me thinking and I'm quick to admit that after discussing the question with numerous expert sailors (many of whom *at first* thought that sailing high in order to lee bow the tide was desirable) I am now certain that the thesis should be qualified.

When approaching a weather mark which you are just not fetching, if your course takes you directly into the current, by pinching slightly the tide will crab your boat to windward and may make it possible to fetch the mark without tacking. True, your boat will slow down somewhat, but if the distance to the mark is slight this loss in speed might be less than the distance which would have been lost by having to make two short tacks in order to fetch the mark. If such is the case, when faced with the choice of whether or not to lee bow the tide, by all means do so.

There are other occasions such as when beating up a narrow channel, or when attempting to round a headland, or when just outside of a helpful back eddy, that pinching *slightly* so as to lee bow the tide will enable you to clear the channel, round the headland or get into the back eddy without making two extra tacks. In such situations, it is up to the skipper to weigh the advantage of lee bowing against the disadvantage of the loss in speed occasioned by pinching slightly and then to act accordingly.

Except in certain specialized situations such as those above, however, it pays to sail your boat just as you would have if no tidal current existed and without worrying about whether or not you are lee bowing it. Lee bowing will, of course, always permit you to make good more to windward but if you must pinch to do so, unless there are other offsetting factors, you will get to the windward mark later. The effect of lee bowing the tide at the cost of pinching, except in instances such as those cited, will not offset the loss in speed caused by pinching.

Tacking for the Mark

Tide alters the position at which one should tack for weather mark. If the tide is against you, it will be necessary to go further to windward in order to lay the mark. Only by apparently overstanding can the leeway of the current be offset. It is disastrous to tack short and try to pinch up against the tide. You will take much longer to do it, may foul the mark or may fail to fetch altogether. Going a length or two too far is good insurance because if you have to bear off for the mark you will travel at great speed. (Fig. 56).

With a fair tide, one should tack for the mark earlier than in slack water because the tide will push the boat to windward. (Fig. 57).

Compensating for Tide on a Reach

On a reach, tide will greatly affect the course made good and this effect must be compensated for. In brief, one steers somewhat in the direction the tide is coming from. Assume a boat speed of six knots and a tide of two knots. Figure 58 shows a few of the courses that must be steered to make good the mark under varying directions of tide. It also shows how tide affects speed.

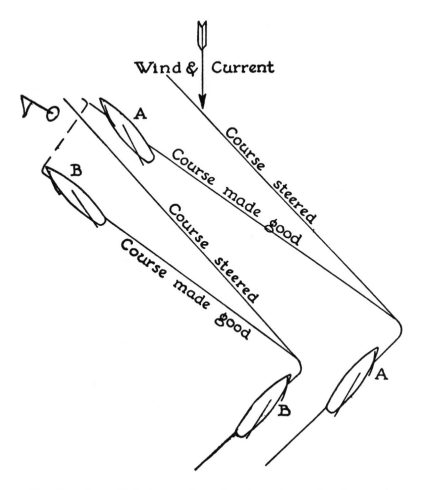

Fig. 56—Boat B fails to allow for the tide setting her to leeward and has to make an extra tack to fetch the mark. A,
compensating properly, rounds first.

Don't Get too Far to Windward in a Fair Tide

When reaching with a tide which is either astern or pushing you to windward, it is particularly important to avoid getting much to windward of the
base course. If you do, it is doubly difficult to come down and the boat must
square away far before the wind in order to do so. In so doing, she loses speed
rapidly. Luffing matches, therefore, must be avoided even more carefully
under such conditions.

When the tide is coming directly against you, it isn't so bad if your boat

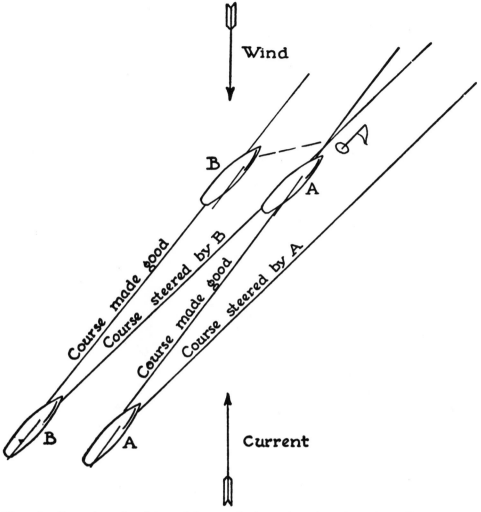

Fig. 57—Boat A tacks short of the mark, knowing that the tide will set her up
enough to fetch the mark and round ahead of B.

gets quite a bit to one side or the other of the course. Since the tide is ahead, there will be more time than otherwise to get back on the course and a less sharp sailing angle is required to do so. Also, as you are sailing at an angle to the current, the boat is crabbed sideways in the fashion that we noted when discussing the effect of lee bowing the tide. This facilitates getting back to the direct course. We conclude, therefore, that in a head tide there is great freedom in the course one can take. Follow the wind pretty much at will, as it is a simple matter to get back to the base course.

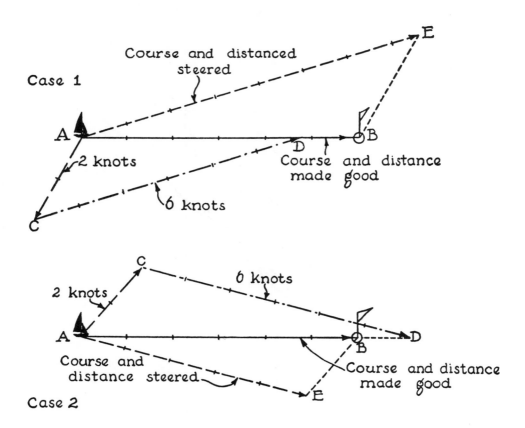

Fig. 58—In both cases 1 and 2, above, a boat at point A is proceeding to mark B. Her speed through the water is 6 knots, the distance to the mark is 6 nautical miles and the speed of the current is 2 knots. To compensate for the current (the direction of which differs in the two cases) draw line AC, two miles long and in the direction of the current. Then, using C as a center and the boat's speed of 6 knots as a radius, swing an arc till it hits the line AB. CD then indicates the *direction* to be steered. Draw AE parallel to CD. This is the course to steer from position A to make good the course AB. By drawing a line from B, parallel to AC until it hits the course steered line at E, one determines the length of AE which indicates the *distance* one must sail to reach mark B.

The Effect of Tide on a Run

While running directly before the wind, tacking down wind becomes doubly effective with a fair tide. This is so for a variety of reasons. First of all, as the boat reaches off the direct dead run course, the tide makes her crab sideways and keeps her closer to the direct course than if there was no tide. Secondly, and of perhaps greater importance, when a boat runs directly before the wind, her speed is subtracted from the speed of the wind and resulting apparent strength of wind is not great. With a fair tide, this apparent wind is reduced even further. In light airs it may get close to nothing. In such cases, the boat is carried largely by the tide and travels *very slowly through the water*. By tacking down wind, the apparent wind is drawn further forward, the sails fill and the boat gains headway through the water. The increase in speed through the water may be tremendous and at the same time the tide is helping as much as ever.

With the tide ahead, tacking down wind becomes less effective than in slack water, and much less than with a fair tide. The tide forces the boat further off the course than normal and it tends to increase the apparent wind of a boat that is running. It does so because her speed over the bottom is slowed down and the wind can stay up with her more easily. Since one of the main advantages of tacking down wind is to increase the boat's speed by increasing a light apparent wind, it follows that when tide has already increased the strength of the apparent wind much of the value of tacking down wind is removed. An exception exists when the course is such that the dead run course heads down the strongest part of the tide. Then, tacking down wind may help by taking the boat out of the strong head tide into a weaker one or possibly even into a fair one.

Tide Can Affect a Boat's Speed Through the Water

We have noted previously that tide affects chiefly the boat's speed over the bottom and not through the water. True, but we have already noted how it can affect a running boat's speed through the water, depending on whether the tide is ahead or astern. The same general rule holds true on all points of sailing, especially when the breeze is light. Whenever the wind is forward of the beam, a fair tide increases the apparent wind and hence increases the boat's speed through the water as well as over the bottom. With the wind forward of the beam, a head tide, by reducing the apparent wind, reduces the boat's speed both over the bottom and through the water. *It follows, therefore, that when the wind is forward of the beam, the effect of tide is doubly important.*

Hence it is more than ever necessary to play the tide right under such conditions.

On the other hand, with wind astern a fair tide decreases apparent wind and, therefore, though it increases the boat's speed over the bottom, it decreases it through the water. A head tide with wind astern increases the apparent wind, and therefore increases the boat's speed through the water at the same time that it decreases it over the bottom. *The obvious conclusion is that when the wind is abaft the beam, the effect of tide is of diminished importance, and the skipper should use less drastic means to reach a fair tide, or to avoid a foul one.*

Tide and a Dying Breeze

In a dying breeze it is best at first to overcompensate for the set of the tide. On a reach, for example, with the tide setting to windward, one would get to leeward of the course. Then, when the wind lightened, the tide would bring you up to the course easily. If to windward of the course as the wind lightened, it would be doubly difficult to get down to the mark.

By the same line of reasoning, in a rising breeze, it is best to take an initial course which will take you nearer to the mark, even though off to one side of it. Don't fight the tide in the light wind. When the breeze increases, it will become a relatively simple matter to get back on the direct course.

In concluding our consideration of the effect of tide on yacht racing, we cannot help but notice that there is a great deal more to it than might meet the casual eye. All to the good—it makes a fascinating sport still more interesting.

XII

Racing in Light and Fluky Winds

LIGHT WINDS, especially when they are fluky too (as they usually are), tax the skill of skipper and crew to the utmost. It is then that the finest touch is needed to coax speed from the boat and the keenest concentration required to choose the proper course. Luck is a factor but less important than may be supposed. Actually, light weather racing calls for the greatest skill of all. Under such conditions, it is easy to sail the course without mishap, but we are interested in getting around it ahead of the other boats and that's a job. Though experience in light airs is the best teacher of all, the observance of certain principles will prove helpful.

The problem divides into two parts, sailing the boat fast and sailing her the right place.

GETTING THE MOST OUT OF THE BOAT

While the purist might argue that it is impossible to sail "fast" in light airs, he must admit that there are ways to improve a boat's speed in such conditions. One of these is through the use of full cut sails. New sails are generally fuller than old ones. With use, the draft of a sail reduces and eventually it becomes best suited to heavy winds. In light air, then, we use one of our newer sails, and, if there are several, we select the one with the greatest draft.

To keep the mainsail full and most effective in light airs, remove most, if not all, of the mast's fore and aft curve. Draft can be further increased by keeping the foot, and especially the luff, of the main a bit slack. By such means, even a flat sail can be given a new lease on life.

Nowadays almost all headsails have stretchy luffs. Therefore draft can be increased in the jib by reducing halliard tension. If done to excess this will produce wrinkles. But often it's better to accept the wrinkles since a fuller sail provides so much extra drive in light air.

139

Use Light Sheets

The use of light weight sheets permits sails to lift and draw more easily in a light breeze. Changing the regular main sheet for a lighter one is risky, since the wind might come up during the race and it might be impossible to reeve in the heavier sheet. A solution that is sometimes practiced on boats with a double ended main sheet is to splice a length of light line into one end of the regular sheet. This line remains coiled up and out of use in average winds. In light airs, it is pulled through the blocks and substituted for the regular main sheet which in turn is coiled up out of the way. Should the wind rise it is a simple matter, even during the race, to overhaul the sheet so that the regular line is again in use. The only disadvantage is that the main sheet must be twice its usual length and this creates a slight stowage problem.

Reduce the Number of Parts

Much the same effect may be achieved by reducing the number of parts of the main sheet. This is achieved by using a snatch block for one of the main sheet leads. In light winds, the block is opened and the sheet bypasses it. (Fig. 59).

The chief advantage from such a rig lies in the fact that the sheet slacks much more readily, its parts are not so prone to drop in the water and the sail is able to lift and flow off to leeward in the light going.

As regards jib sheets for light weather racing, it is a simple matter to detach the regular sheet (and any blocks which may be attached to the clew) and substitute marlin or light nylon line. Should the breeze increase, it is no problem to return to the ordinary sheets. In the meantime, the jib has a greater chance to catch and respond to each passing zephyr. Furthermore, with the heavy sheets and blocks removed, the sail is not so prone to slat about if a sea is running.

Light sheets are even more important on spinnakers. In small boats 1/8" braided nylon flag halliard is ideal. In large boats you will have to go a bit heavier, but still use sheets a great deal lighter than the regular ones. Light sheets allow the spinnaker to lift better and flow out away from the main. They also cause far less shaking of the chute from wave action.

A Light Crew and A Quiet One

A lightweight crew is helpful in soft winds. Weight is not needed for stability; hence the lighter the better. But, there is no guarantee that the wind

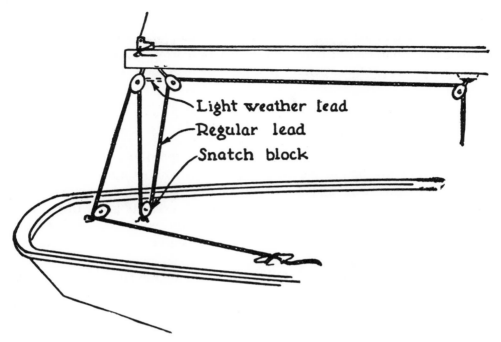

Light weather lead
Regular lead
Snatch block

Fig. 59—A typical rig for reducing the number of main sheet parts in
light weather.

will not increase, and few skippers go so far as changing crews according to
the weather, or leaving one of the regular members ashore. About all that is
recommended, therefore, in this connection is to remember not to ask an extra
guest along for the ride when the wind is light.

It is of far greater importance for the crew to move about as little as
possible. Any movement tends to rock the boat and will shake much of the
wind out of her sails. A sudden movement may change the boat's trim enough
to cut some of her speed that has been built up with painstaking care. In very
light going, enough of the crew should be to leeward to cause the boat to heel.
This enables the sail to assume a more effective shape and allows it to take
advantage of the lightest winds.

In very light going, sheets should be slacked slowly and smoothly. Slacking fast will back the sail and exert a pressure opposed to the boat's advance.
In trimming slightly, the adjustment should also be done slowly, but if one is
making a major trim, such as that required when going from a run to a close
reach, or when trimming for a jibe, pull the main in swiftly. Doing so will fill
the sail and will push the boat forward in the process. In the case of a jibe,
remember, after trimming fast, to push the boom out slowly on the other side.

To keep the mainsail relatively quiet when a sea is running, a forward guy
attached to the main boom is helpful. It keeps the boom from slatting about.

In the absence of such a guy, one of the crew should hold the boom steady whenever an especially large sea is encountered. Whether using a guy or holding the boom, be sure to pull it forward, or to leeward, rather than down. Pulling down tends to harden the leech and reduces the sail's draft.

Sail with a Good Rap Full

By far the most important rule for increasing speed to windward in light airs is to sail with slightly started sheets. Slack them out a few inches more than in an average wind and *don't try to point too high*. The average boat goes best to windward in light airs when pointing 5° or even 10° lower than usual. The added speed much more than makes up for the extra distance that must be sailed. By all means don't pinch—you will starve the boat and get nowhere.

To allow the main to be slacked without sagging too far to leeward (thus hurting pointing ability) the main sheeting base should be pulled to windward, actually to windward of the centerline. Then, when the sheet is eased draft is increased, but the main is not far to leeward of the centerline.

FLUKY WEATHER TACTICS

Of even greater importance than sailing fast in light and fluky winds is the ability to go the right place. Admittedly, luck is a bigger factor under such conditions than in a steady wind. But some skippers manage to remain "lucky" week after week, until finally it becomes apparent that their tactics are really responsible for their continued success. It is significant that the skippers who win in steady winds are often the "lucky" ones in fluky going.

The Start Becomes Less Important

In light and spotty winds, the start is apt to be of diminished importance. Even then, a good start remains a great asset, particularly if the first leg heads into a freshening breeze. But in most cases any initial advantage is far from secure on a fluky day. It is then harder to stay ahead than it is to come from behind, profiting by the leaders' mistakes and sailing around them when they run into a flat spot or choose a poor course. Getting a topnotch start is often risky, inviting the chance of getting over too early or of being involved in a foul on the line. In a steady breeze, the probable gain justifies the risk but, in a spotty wind, a more conservative start will serve nearly as well. We conclude, therefore, that in a light, shifty breeze it is better to play safe at the start, trying to get a *good* one but not taking an undue risk in an effort to beat the fleet.

Think Less of the Boat, More of the Weather

Once the start has been made, it doesn't pay to concentrate too heavily on sailing the boat fast. In a steady breeze, the skipper should watch the sails almost constantly, and the crew should spend most of the time trimming them or keeping low and quiet if going to windward. This should make her go faster. But when the wind is apt to shift every few minutes, it seems more important to be going a little slower in the right direction than rapidly in the wrong one. Consequently, the skipper should spend less time watching the sails and more watching the weather, deducing where the next puff is apt to come from, in order to be there when it does. The crew shouldn't be idle either. Even when on the wind, it is a good idea for the one with the best eyesight and the best knowledge of weather to keep looking about to see what's going on. When he sees a puff of smoke on shore coming from a different direction, distant sails filled with a new slant, or a line of breeze making up on the horizon, he can call the skipper's attention to it without pointing; then plans can be changed to make the most of the new breeze when it sets in.

The Importance of Tide Is Diminished

The importance of tide diminishes as the breeze becomes more uncertain. In a steady light breeze, tide would be more important than in a steady heavy one, but light airs are all too often fickle as well. In a good wind, when shifts of more than half a point or so are unlikely, the difference between a fair and a foul tide can often more than offset the difference between a good or bad slant. This is less often the case in spotty going. The flukier the wind, the greater the advantage that can be gained by getting the best slants. Therefore, under such conditions, the course which will lead to better breezes, even if it results in a less favoring current, is apt to be the faster one. In places such as Vineyard Haven, where the tide is especially strong, it is, at almost all times, the primary consideration. We might suggest, however, that such a place is the exception which proves the rule.

Which Course to Sail?

With the wind shifting and coming in "all over the lot," it is difficult to count on anything too far in advance. Long range plans should be discarded or altered to meet the new situation. On a steady day, one should figure out the best tack, if beating, and the best course, if running free, and stick to it as long as the wind remains about the same. Lack of persistence often results in a middle position. Under less predictable conditions, however, such persistence is not always wise. Even then, when distant smoke, a cloud formation, or a line of breeze on the water gives a good indication of what is going to happen, a continued tack over into the expected breeze is probably the best bet, even though small "headers" are encountered en route. Also, local knowledge or weather bureau information may make it justifiable to play one side or the other. But in the absence of these clues, no one can decide with any degree of certainty where the breeze will come from. The best one can do, in such a case, is to decide on the best tack *for the moment*. If a "header" comes, it is best to tack rather than plug after an imaginary breeze which might not be there when you get to it. By thus taking advantage of present favors, you are continually getting closer to the mark than someone who sticks on the one board hoping for a major break.

This method of sailing from minute to minute in spotty going may not result in quite as many wins as taking a long chance off to one side. It will, though, bring many firsts, assure many good positions, and will seldom result in a bad setback—the greatest peril on a fluky day.

Don't Chase Another's Advantage

If, however, someone a short distance to windward of you gets a good slant, it is unwise to tack over into it, *unless there is a good lift to carry you over to it*. In a steady breeze, the advantage another boat gains is apt to be permanent and it is often wise to take one's medicine, sail over behind this boat with the idea that, once there, you may work up and surely will do better than staying where you were. On fluky days, this seldom pays because, by the time you get over to the good breeze, it has often petered out. If such is the case, you will find yourself much worse off than if you had never chased the wind. You have been going slowly while chasing it and are hopelessly behind the boats that had it. Furthermore, those boats which you did have astern before tacking may also have passed you, since they were taking advantage of a momentary lift while you were trying in vain to reach a still better one. Of course, if a breeze of any permanence appears, then it is best to get to it even if you lose momentarily. Otherwise, make the most of what you have and if, by so doing, you can also head for a breeze that promises to be even stronger, so much the better. If not, it is best to stay where you are, relying on the law of averages to bring the next break your way. A boat that spends all afternoon chasing the advantages of others is never in a position to get any of her own.

Tactics for the Leading Boat

The leading boat is faced with the question to cover or not to cover. In a steady breeze, the boat which has worked out a nice lead in the first part of the race should cover the bunch, or at least her nearest competitors, thereafter. At first thought, one is apt to conclude that on a fluky day this tactic is more in order than ever, so that one may play extra safe. But it doesn't work out that way in practice. In a small fleet of three or four boats, it may be possible to cover them all, and this should be done in even the most fickle winds. Once in a while, nine-tenths of a large fleet goes the same way; if such is the case, the leading boat should cover—no matter what her skipper's opinion as to the best place to go. As a rule, however, the fleet divides and boats are going in both directions. Now, to get between the bulk of the fleet and the mark, it is necessary to sail a predetermined course. We have already tried to point out that, on a fluky day, unless there are indications which give reliable information about the best tack to take, the fastest courses are not predetermined but are regulated by the wind at the moment. A middle course, therefore, unless the shifts make it also the fastest, should not be attempted. If you do try a middle course, the boats astern which have tacked only on the good slants or which have headed for some good breeze on the horizon, become a threat.

Boats will be as much as a mile on either side. You have come as close as possible to cover them all but this is still not very close. In the great majority of cases, the boat on one side or the other will go past the boat in the center. At times, I've even seen fleets on both sides go by, each getting a favoring slant on different tacks while the hapless boat in the middle is in a dead spot between them.

This happens too often to be exceptional. Usually, if, instead of trying in vain to cover both sides of the fleet, you take advantage of the winds or head for a major shift which you have fairly reliable reasons to expect, you will find that the best boats in the fleet will be doing the same thing and you will be covering them anyway. And, if in this process, you happen to get off to one side, you can be sure of beating all the boats on that side rather than running the risk of being stuck in the middle with both halves of the fleet sailing past.

It seems true that not only do more wins result from not consciously covering the fleet on fluky days, but that fewer flops result.

It is perhaps even less advisable to cover the two or three closest boats on·a fluky day. In such conditions, winds shift so quickly and to such a degree that not a single boat can be safely counted out. In a steady wind, if the nearest boats can be kept astern, the others, even if they do get some small advantage from a slightly better wind, will not gain enough to pass the leader. If, however, in spotty going, you focus all your attention on the closest contenders at the moment, the others are apt to slip by. A 200-yard lead over the bulk of the fleet is not the safe margin it is under steadier conditions, and every boat should be considered a threat. It seems best, therefore, to sail what is considered the fastest course; if the second and third boats follow, so much the better. Of course, if you are approaching the finish or one of the turning marks, then it is best to cover the nearest competitors.

Tactics for the Boats Behind

Suppose that in the first half of the race everything has gone wrong and you find yourself behind most of the boats. In a steady breeze, splitting tacks with the fleet seldom works since most of the boats are apt to be going the right place. Splitting tacks under such conditions works occasionally, but more often it results in a last or, at least, a bad dumping. At such times, it seems best, especially if your boat is a fast one, to plug after the fleet, overhauling a few and beating those which, with less patience than yourself, hoped for a miracle and tacked the wrong way.

In variable weather, it is far more desirable to split with the fleet unless there is some breeze that they are obviously heading into. When conditions are uncertain, just because most of the boats are going the same way is no guarantee they are sailing the best course. The chances are that they have a pretty hazy idea themselves just why they are on the tack they have chosen. Consequently, the last boat, instead of taking a ten to one chance when splitting tacks, has an almost even one of getting the best slant.

Yachtsmen often behave like sheep, following a leader who has a reputation. This is just what he wants as he can then cover them easily. Unless the place he is going is obviously better than another, you are more of a threat to him when you split tacks or change your tactics so as not to just follow him.

Tactics Off Wind

While running and reaching in light airs, it is more than ever necessary to work to leeward in the puffs. In very light going, speed is increased tremendously by sharpening up closer to the wind. This is called freshening your wind. In order to be able to do this and still average the course, it is imperative to bear off below it in the puffs, however slight the increase in wind might be.

On a run, tacking down wind becomes increasingly effective as the wind lightens. It is possible to sail 30° *or more* off the course and still make up for the extra distance by the resulting increase in speed. When tacking down wind, the skipper should plan his course to stay in wind streaks as long as possible and to take advantage of wind shifts. If a shift occurs which will enable the boat to sail just as close to the wind on the opposite jibe and yet come closer to the direct course, then a jibe is in order.

When all is said and done, it must be admitted that it's a tough job to win constantly in light and fluky going. But, it need not be as hard as might be supposed. If the boat is sailed fast and sound tactics are followed, it is seldom that really bad luck will come your way.

XIII

Racing in a Heavy Wind

RACING IN A STRONG wind and heavy sea may lack some of the subtlety of light weather racing but more than makes up for it in added thrills and excitement. To win under such conditions requires skill of a somewhat different sort. Tactics remain of definite importance but are subordinate to sailing the boat at high speed, and keeping her from capsizing, filling up or carrying away the rig.

Use a Flat Sail

A prerequisite to sailing fast to windward in heavy weather is a flat sail. As a sail grows older, its draft is reduced, and it becomes better suited to heavy weather. Old ones eventually become blown out—their draft shifts too far aft or they become *too* flat. Such a sail lacks drive and is slow even in the strongest wind. So don't necessarily select the oldest and flattest sail for heavy going. Do choose a flat one, but don't go to extremes. If you are sailing in unprotected waters you will need enough draft to punch through the big seas. In protected waters a very flat sail is the answer.

We have noted in a previous chapter that sails can be made more efficient in heavy weather by curving the mast to reduce draft. Star boats have demonstrated the extremes to which this may be done. But in these boats, as in all others, it is possible to bend the mast too far, reducing the draft too much and inviting mast failure to boot. Experience alone can tell when the proper bend has been imparted.

The Question of Reefing

In winds of 20 knots or stronger, many boats sail faster with a reefed main. Some go faster with full sail, but these are the exception. Full sail under such conditions overpowers the average boat, makes her heel excessively (even with

148

much of the main aback), carry a strong weather helm and slows her down. Strangely, a reefed sail is frequently faster on reaches and runs as well as on the wind. The explanation lies in the fact that under extreme conditions an unreefed main tends to bury the boat's bow while running. She is over-powered, often unmanageable and staggers on at slower speed than the more conservatively canvassed boat.

Before the race, if in doubt whether to reef, it is wiser to decide in favor of doing so. After the start, if one discovers that the full sail boats are faster, it is possible to shake out the reef without losing much ground. Even with a good crew and jiffy reefing a bit more distance is lost tieing in a reef, partly because your crew will be unable to hike while reefing. In deciding whether or not to reef, however, don't think only of the strength of the puffs. Frequently, on a puffy day, a reefed boat is a bit faster in the puffs but a great deal slower in the lulls between. Reefing at its best usually results in only a slight increase in speed and at its worst in a very great decrease. Of course, if the puffs are so strong that the boat is apt to capsize or lose her mast, a reef is certainly in order.

In very strong winds, the spinnaker becomes of less importance and even-tually can slow the boat down. This is especially true on a reach. As the wind increases, it must come correspondingly farther aft for the spinnaker to be carried to advantage. In extreme conditions, except in boats with a planing type of hull, a spinnaker may slow the boat down even on a dead run. Displacement type boats have a maximum speed and all efforts to drive them faster merely result in overpowering them and burying the bow. In all boats, there comes a time when, for reasons of safety, the spinnaker can no longer be carried. If, while running under such conditions, the boat becomes unman-ageable, winging out the jib to windward is sure to make her balance better and steer more easily. In boats that can plane or surf it often pays to be bold and carry the chute.

The jib should almost always be carried while racing. The only exception might be in winds so strong (above 35 knots) that the race should not have been started. When sailing to windward in heavy going, the jib is the most effective sail and furnishes the greater part of the drive. Some boats which have both genoa and working jibs find that even in winds of 30 knots the genoa and a reefed and luffing mainsail provide the fastest combination. True, the big jib will be harder to handle, and it may be too risky to carry, but it is *sometimes* faster, even though its use necessitates carrying a still greater luff in the mainsail.

Sail the Boat on Her Feet

More important than the right combination of sails is the manner of sailing. In brief, the boat should be sailed "on her feet." Never permit the lee rail to bury more than an inch or so, even in keel boats. Boats with high freeboard may go faster with the rail always above water, and centerboard boats must be sailed flatter still. Heeling past a certain point increases the weather helm and reduces drive, since the wind slips over the top of the sail. The boat no longer sails on her designed lines; she wallows, goes slowly, and makes excessive leeway because her keel or centerboard is so far from vertical.

But how to keep the boat from heeling too much while beating in a heavy blow? Contrary to popular belief, *not* by easing the main sheet. This only necessitates bearing off in order to retain any drive and even though the main carries a luff, the broader angle to the wind tends to heel the boat excessively. Instead of slacking the main, keep it trimmed flat, push the boom to leeward (if on a traveller, bridle or athwartship blocking) and point higher. By feathering up in this manner, the boat not only points higher, but actually foots faster than one which is overpowered and carrying an extreme luff.

In especially severe puffs it may be necessary to ease the main suddenly to prevent a capsize or to keep from laying over despite your best efforts to feather. To permit quick releasing, have the main cleated to a cam cleat. If the skipper or one of the crew has the hauling part in his hand, the main can be released in a split second. There is no need even in centerboard boats to keep the main uncleated, provided cams are used and in fact without them it's virtually impossible keep the sheet trimmed flat enough. As soon as the first blast of the puff has passed, retrim and resume feathering. On larger boats a jig or a winch on one end of the main sheet is recommended to expedite retrimming.

It is especially important to keep the jib full in strong breezes. Therefore trim it real flat. In heavy seas it may have to be eased slightly and the boat headed off *slightly* to impart more drive. In smooth water it is almost impossible to overtrim the jib in a strong breeze. Except on small boats, therefore, good jib sheet winches are a must. Only in a fierce blast and then only for survival, should the jib be let fly.

Hiking is another means of keeping the boat from heeling too much. Skipper and crew should get as far to windward as possible (remaining low in the process). An agile crew may be able to hang out over the windward rail so that much of his body is beyond and *below* the weather rail. If yours can, so much the better, as everything which contributes to stability increases speed in dusty going. A heavy crew and a large one is a real advantage as the wind increases. But remember that in ocean racers it is illegal to have the torso of any crew member outside of the lifelines.

More valuable than a heavy crew is one that is trained to work together smoothly and without orders. There is apt to be so much noise and confusion in heavy weather that it may be impossible for the skipper to direct the crew or impossible for them to hear him if he did.

Even with a light crew, stability can be increased by stowing all movable gear as low as possible. Any extra sails or equipment should be stowed on the floor boards (beneath them when practicable). Don't hesitate to take plenty of equipment on a windy day. The increase in weight is actually beneficial under such conditions, providing it is stowed properly.

Keep the Boat Dry

It is of the greatest importance to keep the boat "dry" in heavy going. Spray enters the cockpit from the windward side and water is apt to slop in to leeward. This water must not be allowed to accumulate. Of course some boats have self-bailing cockpits, and most modern racing boats have suction bailers, which if left open can bail water out even when sailing to windward. If yours doesn't, be sure to have a good hand pump or small bucket, and have the lightest crew member bail as fast as possible when water accumulates. It doesn't take much water to add appreciably to the boat's weight, and it is harmful weight, since it seeks the leeward side and thus buries the boat instead of adding to her stability. The free surface effect of the water sloshing about, whether on a beat, a reach or a run, reduces stability further.

Once the race begins, it is impossible to avoid taking in lots of spray and some water may enter to leeward. Bailing then becomes the chief remedy.

By far the best way to bail is to equip your boat with suction bailers. They are easy for a professional builder to install, remain tight when not in use, and really suck the water out as soon as the boat is up to four or five knots of speed. They were originally intended for use on downwind legs, but most modern racing boats go fast enough to make them work upwind. If you let the boat stall out, water will come in. The remedy is to drive off a bit to pick up speed. Even if you lose a bit to weather you will soon be free of water and able to resume normal sailing. If water still comes in through the bailers, close them until enough water has accumulated to warrant reopening them and driving off again.

Some modern boats have transom flaps that work in much the same way as suction bailers. One way or another you must keep the boat dry! Self-bailers are worth their weight in gold on all boats that don't have self-bailing cockpits.

Running and Reaching in a Strong Wind

So far, our discussion has referred mostly to sailing fast to windward. Many observations apply equally to reaching. The boat must still be sailed on her feet. While reaching in a strong wind, if you become overpowered, releasing the vang can be helpful. This spills wind from the upper part of the main and enables the boat to get back on her feet. It is essential to have a powerful vang so you can retrim easily in the first lull. Release of the vang is especially useful to avoid broaching. In very strong winds, after releasing the vang, it is important to carry a big luff in the main. Weather helm is usually at its worst on a reach and an eased main is the most effective way to reduce it. It is a very common fault to trim the main too flat while reaching. Just because the lee rail is clear of the water is no guarantee that the sail is not trimmed too flat. If the weather helm is strong, the chances are the boat will go faster with the main eased more. Give it a try. As on the wind, the jib must remain full. On a dead run, ease the main as far as it can go.

The crew should get as far to windward as they can but there is no longer any advantage in them keeping low. With wind abaft the beam, windage is no longer harmful, so the crew may sit up and assume positions most effective for trimming the sails and seeing what is going on. Their weight should be shifted somewhat aft of the best position for beating.

When on top of a wave, the skipper should bear off with it somewhat and ride to leeward on it as long as possible. Furthermore, relatively flat, light displacement boats can often gain stability on a reach by heading off wind and planing. This is most noticeable in the inland lake scow type where it is accepted practice to bear away instead of luffing when in danger of capsizing while reaching. In between seas, head up above the course in order to be ready to ride down the next sea.

If the bow starts to bury while running or reaching, a quick, short luff is usually sufficient to lift the bow out of the wave. This is risky in a light centerboard boat, since the sudden course change may capsize her, but it is better than sailing her under.

Safety Precautions

The observance of certain precautions should prevent mishaps in heavy weather. Replace worn rigging before starting out and inspect standing rigging to see that it is all in good order.

Never belay the main sheet except in a cam cleat. It must be free to run in case of a knockdown puff. If you don't have cams, a few turns on the cleat with a slipping hitch are O.K., but not so many that the sheet cannot be slacked instantly. To get the best speed out of the boat in a reach in particular, it is necessary for the main sheet to be tended. Slack it out before the puffs and take back what you have given when the puff has passed. The jib sheet can be belayed except in the strongest blows, at which time it too should be secured only by a turn or two and held by one member of the crew. Never lash the tiller or obstruct it in any way. The halliards must be cleated, of course, but don't half-hitch them. They may have to come down in a hurry and a half hitch, especially after it gets wet, may be hard to cast loose. Use a slip hitch.

It is plain common sense for each member of the crew to wear a life jacket in very heavy weather. If the boat should capsize, stay with her as long as she is afloat. If she is a keel boat and sinks, be careful to avoid getting a foot caught in a sheet or other line. Mark the boat's position by ranges on shore so that she can be salvaged later.

TACTICS

Tactics for heavy weather racing are much the same as those for moderate conditions, but with a few notable exceptions.

Don't Tack Down Wind

Tacking down wind in displacement type boats is out. On a dead run it might be necessary, but avoid doing so if you can. The only advantage to be gained by tacking down wind in normal conditions is the added speed a boat gains on a reach. In a strong wind, she is at her maximum speed and hence the shortest course is the best. In light displacement hulls, however, and particularly in scow types, there are still advantages in tacking to leeward, since the boats have practically no maximum speed. Often one can reach off and stay on a wave, thus surfboarding at the speed of the wave which may travel as fast as 15 knots.

Avoid Jibes

Jibes should be avoided, whenever possible. No matter how skillfully executed, they involve some risk of carrying away the mast as the sail swings over. In a very heavy wind it may be absolutely impossible to jibe without capsizing or running an unwarranted risk of damaging the boat. Under such conditions, when on a run, bear off to leeward of the course as much as possible in the comparative lulls in the wind. During the puffs it may be imperative to head up a bit above the course in order to spill some wind from the sails and keep the boat from swamping, or to avoid a broach to windward. Boats can and do capsize through being overpowered on a run and shaking some of the wind from the sails is the best way to prevent this. If you fail to get below the course when you can, and a strong puff strikes just before reaching the mark, it may be impossible to hold the boat off enough to round the mark. Since a jibe is out of the question in such going, one's only recourse is to go about, thus losing so much ground that the race, to all intents and purposes, is as good as lost. (Fig. 60).

It is only under the most extreme conditions, however, that a boat cannot be jibed, provided the maneuver is executed properly. The trick is to have several men on the main sheet so that the sail can be brought in fast and controlled as it fills on the other side. The boat must never lose speed.

Avoid Jams

In a heavy wind and sea, avoid close contact with the other boats. At the start, in jams at the marks and whenever other boats are near, give them a wider berth than usual. Under such conditions, boats are less maneuverable and may become unmanageable. Collisions can occur easily, and if they do, the result is apt to be serious, due to the greater force of impact.

The same rule applies to giving marks a slightly wider berth. It isn't necessary to leave them far off, but don't skin them as close as you would in moderate going. If you do, a sea or a vicious puff may force you against the mark and throw you out of the race.

Get into Smooth Water

It is helpful to choose a tack which takes you in the lee of the shore, especially while beating against a strong wind. In the more protected waters, waves will be smaller and the sea smoother. The boat will go faster than those further off shore that are bucking into larger seas.

Make Few Tacks

It is well to avoid frequent tacks during a heavy wind. Each time the boat comes about, the heavy seas bring her to an almost dead stop and considerable distance is lost. Some boats will have difficulty tacking at all and these run the risk of "getting in irons" and being unable to fill away and get moving on the new tack. Even if the tack is accomplished without mishap, there is danger of her capsizing or filling up just after she has filled away on the new tack. She is nearly dead in the water and unable to respond to her helm in case of a

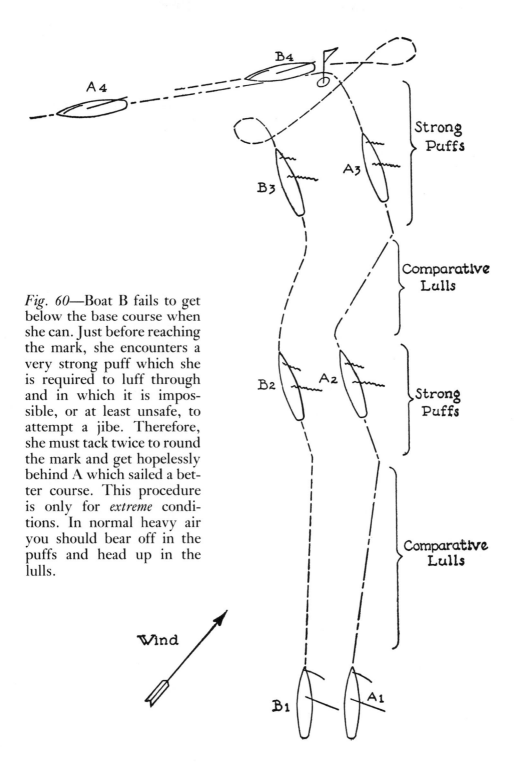

Fig. 60—Boat B fails to get below the base course when she can. Just before reaching the mark, she encounters a very strong puff which she is required to luff through and in which it is impossible, or at least unsafe, to attempt a jibe. Therefore, she must tack twice to round the mark and get hopelessly behind A which sailed a better course. This procedure is only for *extreme* conditions. In normal heavy air you should bear off in the puffs and head up in the lulls.

particularly heavy puff. Unable to luff, her only recourse is to slack sheets. This may prevent capsizing, but it also postpones the time when headway is gained on the new tack. If wind shifts make frequent tacks desirable, wait for comparative lulls in the wind in which to come about.

A win on a windy day is doubly sweet, because you will have licked not only your competitors but the winds and waves too.

XIV

Sailing Planing Boats
and Catamarans

As an active racing man knows, in the last decade there has been quite a trend toward planing boats, boats which in strong winds and on down wind legs can skim over the water rather than sailing through it. In the past few years catamarans have also become increasingly popular. In many respects, both of these types are sailed just like any other boat, and in almost every case, the tactics remain the same. However, there are certain special techniques for getting the most out of both types and hence consideration of these techniques seems in order.

SAILING PLANING BOATS

In light airs, a planing boat is sailed very much the same as heavier keel boats or heavy centerboarders. It becomes even more important, however, in boats of this type to stay quiet under such conditions because, being light, it is easier to shake wind out of the sails.

Up wind, even in strong breezes, the planing boat is once again sailed pretty much like any type. It is, however, even more important to hike efficiently to keep them on their feet and to develop sufficient power so that they can be driven through heavy seas despite their light weight. Scows are an exception to this because they should always be sailed at a considerable angle of heel when going to windward, thus reducing wetted surface and giving the immersed area a long knife-like shape which can slice through the seas.

The Leeward Leg Assumes New Importance

It's when sailing down wind in a strong breeze that planing boats do require special techniques. If you can get one of these boats planing, you can

157

literally double speed over one which is not planing. It's important for the skipper to keep an eye cocked to windward to see puffs approaching. Just as the puff hits, the sails should be trimmed slightly and the boat brought on a closer reach to further increase the strength of the apparent wind. At this time, the entire crew hikes to keep the boat truly on her feet. As speed starts to increase, sheets must be trimmed more as the apparent wind draws further forward. Just the reverse procedure is recommended if the boat is already planing and a puff comes along. Bear off a bit and ease sheets slightly to keep her on her feet.

When on a run, jibing in the lifts is always important, doubly so on a catamaran or planing centerboarder because a great increase in speed can be gained by planing on a reach instead of running dead downwind.

Using the waves to best advantage is also essential. After speed has been increased almost to the point of planing by the procedure outlined above, the skipper waits until the face of a wave has just reached his transom then jerks his tiller up to bear off and run down the wave. Crew weight must, at this instant, be shifted aft quickly. At the same instant it is usually desirable to give a good jerk on the main sheet to give her a momentary shot in the arm. Provided the puff is strong enough the boat will now be planing and said plane can be carried often for hundreds of yards. To keep her planing it's important that the crew weight be always in the right spot. If the bow starts to bury, the crew should get even further aft. If the puff starts to slacken so that with this crew weight aft she starts to drag her transom, weight should ease forward. Unless sailing in a strong breeze, even the best of planing boats will eventually fall off the plane. At this time, the helmsman immediately sharpens up to regain speed, crew weight gets more amidships and when the next puff and wave combination is right, the plane can be regained. This procedure will often keep you on the plane in the comparative lulls.

Make Continual Adjustments

The important point is that continual adjustments, both in course and weight, must be made and said adjustments are often made more suddenly than in conventional boats and to a greater degree. We have already noted that it pays in almost all boats to go up in the light stuff and off in the puffs. In planing boats this is even more pronounced. Often the boat can be made to plane by jerking movements, both of the tiller and sudden shifts of weight. This seems to break her clear of the water and get her on top. To get her started on a plane the crew can often jerk his weight forward, a procedure called ooching. This gives the boat a momentary surge and if this is enough to get her planing the crew must then be quick to shift his weight aft. All of this has to be done at the same time that one is hiking in order to give the needed power. Once on a plane, a boat develops considerable stability since the water becomes hard and produces unusual lift, just as water skis at speed can support a heavy man whereas at lower speed they will sink.

Pumping the Main

Rhythmic pumping of the main sheet is also particularly effective on planing boats. The rub is it must be done at the right time and in conjunction with the waves. Otherwise it will do more harm than good. In the hands of a master, however, one can literally pump a boat on to a plane or even if not truly planing can gain added speed.

By combining these various maneuvers one can wiggle his way down wind in great fashion and in boats of this type the leeward legs assume every bit as much, and in some cases, more importance than the windward ones.

SAILING CATAMARANS

When catamarans first became popular a while ago, many people felt that they required an entirely different sailing technique, both from planing boats and conventional boats. This is not altogether true. Actually they are sailed very much like any other boat but with certain refinements. Upwind in light air and particularly in the smooth seas that usually accompany light air, they are sailed very much like a conventional boat. They can be made to point just about as high with advantage. Down wind under such conditions, it is essential to tack down wind at a greater angle than in a monohull since the increased speed by doing so is accentuated in cats. This applies in strong winds too.

Point Lower in Strong Winds

In stronger breezes, however, the special characteristics of catamarans demand somewhat different handling. When sailing to windward, a catamaran can point just as high as a conventional boat, even in strong breezes, and probably go just as fast. Doing so, however, would fail to take advantage of the great speed that cats can gain and it's for that reason that one sees cats sailing often as much as a point lower than other boats when beating to windward in a breeze. By sailing lower, they can gain as much as 50% extra speed at the expense of perhaps 10% extra distance sailed, obviously a good exchange. The important point is to bear off enough to gain this extra speed without getting carried away by the exhilaration of sailing fast and going even lower than necessary. The trick seems to be to bear off almost as far as a close reach, get her up to really high speed and then start winding her up closer to the wind. When speed has been obtained, the cat can usually be brought up to within a half point of a conventional boat without losing speed. The point comes, however, when speed does start to diminish and it is important at this instant to bear off again immediately, to keep speed on her, and then start winding back up again slowly. It is a question of feel and timing and when you've got a cat in the groove under such conditions it's a grand type to sail.

Use Care in Tacking

Tacking catamarans can be difficult if one isn't careful. The modern ones can tack quite readily but because they have two hulls to bring around and because they are very light and have very little carry, improper execution will get you in irons. To prevent this, watch the seas and time your tack so that you are coming around in a relatively smooth spot rather than punching up against a sea which will stop her quite dead. As the helm is put down and the boat starts to swing up, trim the main flat as a board. This will help her around. As soon as she is head to wind, if there seems to be little carry left and any danger of not completing the tack the crew must be ready to back the jib to bring her around. This is generally not necessary but one must be alert to back the jib at a moment's notice. Once filled away on the tack, it's important for the jib to be trimmed at once and for the main to be eased. The skipper should bear off to a close reach to gain speed as fast as possible, retrimming the main only after she's truly under way.

The Importance of Hiking

Despite the fact that catamarans will not heel appreciably unless they are about ready to capsize, hiking is of tremendous importance. Hiking will keep the leeward hull from burying. The weather hull should never raise too far above the water. It's desirable to have it just licking the tips of the waves but once it gets too airborne it means the leeward one is burying more than necessary and also means that you are riding a risky type tight rope and in continual danger of a capsize. So hike on a cat just as you would on a conventional centerboarder. Failure to do so will not only put you in danger of capsizing but will rob the boat of power.

Down Wind Technique

When sailing a cat downwind the procedure is similar to sailing planing boats. But it's even more important to keep the weight aft. Almost all catamarans have very fine bow sections with little inherent power in them. It's important to keep this bow from burying and this can best be achieved by moving well aft and hiking. We have noted that in the planing boat once on a plane it pays to bear off and ride with the sea. In catamarans this sometimes and frequently is desirable but at other times consider the possibility of heading up in the puffs to gain even greater speeds. The cat has such a very high potential that she might hit truly fantastic speeds by heading up. For example, one would normally be content with say 15 knots broad reaching in a puff but in the same puff the catamaran might hit 20 knots or more if held a point or so higher. It's important to keep in mind that sometimes she has to get down and hence this heading up in puffs should certainly not be overdone. On a run, however, it's apt to be particularly effective because one would then jibe over. Tacking downwind in conventional boats works usually only in very light air but on a catamaran it can be often effective in strong breezes.

Because of their high top speed, it's even more important to be alert to trimming as a catamaran gains speed. Failure to do this will result in the sails luffing as the apparent wind draws forward. Ooching does not seem particularly effective in catamarans largely because they are not true planing types. And hence it's not necessary to break them clear of the water and get them up on top. in fact, ooching can have an adverse effect by burying the leeward hull and by shaking the wind out of the sails. Cats do plane to a degree but despite their fantastic speeds they still sail pretty much through the water, gaining their speed by a combination of great power and a long knife-like hull which offers very little resistance.

Just as in planing boats, catamarans make the leeward legs exciting and rewarding and the type seems destined to increase even more in popularity. They certainly will not replace the conventional boats but do seem destined to supplement them, just as sports cars have not and will not replace sedans but do have real appeal.

XV

Distance Racing Tactics

"GET A FAST BOAT, equip her well, set your course, trim the sails right and let her go. If she's faster and luckier than the others, she will win." That's an overstatement of a feeling some day-racing sailors, and even a few distance racing men, have about long distance racing. True, there are fewer tactics per mile, but over the course of a long race there are one whale of a lot of decisions to be made. While *Finisterre* was a fast boat, anyone who ever raced against her knows she didn't win three straight Bermuda Races on speed alone.

Before considering the tactics of distance racing it must be emphasized that, important as sound tactics are, they won't do much good unless certain basic steps have been taken first. It is, for example, of the greatest importance to line up a top crew, one combining experience with muscle, and above all, one with an abundance of fine helmsmen. And don't overlook the cook—the greatest morale builder or wrecker on any long race.

Of course, the boat must be well equipped, be in top condition, have plenty of spare gear. Above all, however, she must have a gang on board which has the will to win all through the race, which never lets up, which sets sails without hesitation whenever needed, reefs, unreefs without delay and thereby makes the seconds mount to minutes saved by the race's end. If each watch is imbued with the spirit of striving to gain an extra 100 yards each hour, this means well over a mile a day or anything from 40 minutes to two hours saved in a 600-mile race—often a winning margin.

But these factors, important as they are, are far from the whole story. It is here that tactics take over.

Tactics Start Before the Race

The days and weeks before the race are the time to plan your basic course. Read up on past races to find what basic course puts the odds in your favor and to get an idea of what weather conditions might dictate a departure from the favorite course. Also before the race, if it's a coastal race in strong tidal areas, mark up a current chart with the hours of each day the race will last. Thus the crew can look at the current chart and tell at once what the current is at that moment without having to enter the tables.

Study the weather pattern for the few days before the start—this will often give you a clue as to what's coming up next. In the Honolulu Race, which I've not yet sailed, I'm told how vitally important it is to have a good meteorologist on board. The study he makes of present conditions in order to ascertain future ones applies to other races too, and should always start well before the race to give a pattern. To cite a simple example—on the Atlantic seaboard, a nor'easter often lasts three days, swings to sou'west, west or nor'-west on the fourth day. There is nothing exact in this pattern but if you started without knowing how long the easterly had been blowing, you would be at a disadvantage.

In the Bermuda Race, the position of the Gulf Stream should be clearly marked across the rhumb line. This information is now furnished just before the start by the Woods Hole Oceanographic Institution, and the area of most favorable current should have great bearing on the course you set.

The Importance of the Start

Starting tactics may seem unimportant in a race which will last anywhere from overnight to a matter of weeks but even in the longest race it's important to get a good start. Pay particular attention to keeping your wind clear. If you are a minute late and thereby blanketed it may be an hour before you have a completely clear wind, and this could mean a loss of 10 or 15 minutes. There is no single hour in the race when you stand to gain or lose as much as the hour right after the start. Sure you can clear your wind in far less than an hour, but can you do so and still go just where you want to?

It's also a psychological lift to the whole crew if you get a good start—it fires everyone up to get everything possible out of the boat. Conversely, a poor start can have a dampening effect that may take a long time to get over. I remember one Block Island Race in which a good start literally saved us hours some 70 miles later! We broke on top at the start, were able at once to go on the right tack and open up an early lead by being first into a new breeze. Seventy miles later we eased through the Gut just before the flood tide hit us. We were the last boat to get through before the wind died and boats which were still the same half-mile behind us that they were an hour after the start were soon dropped out of sight astern.

Another time it worked just the other way and it so happened that time our start hadn't been so hot. You never know just how important a start, or getting spinnaker on first, etc., may eventually become. In the Honolulu

Race, for example, a good start might get you clear of Catalina sooner and into fresher breezes earlier, thus stretching a small jump into a good margin.

Shortly after the start, set the watches. The off watch should then turn in or take it easy. Even in a 50-mile overnight race it's well to have watches. Perhaps no one will get any sleep but by taking it easy when off watch, you will be keener and more on the ball when you're on. If you have a number of good helmsmen on each watch, rotate at the helm every hour or half-hour on a long race. If it's just an overnight race, the best helmsman aboard should steer for longer periods, but in an ocean race constant switching helps keep everyone more alert.

What Course to Steer?

Once you're started and have clear wind, set out on your predetermined course watching, of course, for any new weather conditions that would indicate a modification in the course. In a short race you would give some thought to covering. In a long one, don't, provided you're convinced your course is best. If, however, you find yourself going it alone, better review the decisions which prompted you to select your course.

If behind early in a long race, just keep plugging along on the "right" course, even if you are following everyone else. There will be ample time to split with the fleet later, so always wait until a split gives promise of bearing fruit.

In a fast boat, it makes particular sense to take the course which seems to offer the best odds. In a boat which has been somewhat outclassed, in order to win it will be wise to leave the fleet *some time* during the race *but wait until a logical time to do so.* There is no sense in getting hopelessly behind early in the race by splitting just for the sake of splitting. That's gambling against the odds, and is not sound tactics.

We've been talking a lot about courses. One might ask, "Except on a beat, is there much choice? Isn't it pretty obvious that a straight line is the shortest distance between two points?" Sure, but often not the fastest.

When beating, of course, you've got a real choice. If it's a dead beat the tack chosen should be that on which you expect to be headed eventually, due to your forecast of weather. If it's a long and a short leg, however, the basic tactic is to take the tack which brings you closest to the mark. If you get let up you may fetch. If headed you can then tack and cross the boats which went off first on the other tack. And all the time you're getting closer to the finish. See Figs. 61 and 62.

This is all pretty basic stuff. What makes winners is the ability to deviate

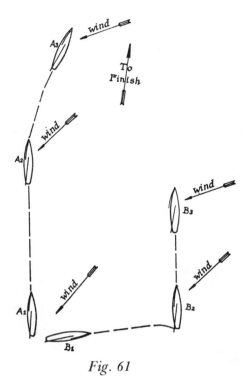

Fig. 61

from the basic tactic at the right time. In the 1952 Bermuda Race in *Revonoc*, we were in great shape 100 miles from the finish. We were up with many larger boats and our chief worry at the time was *White Mist*, which was about 200 yards ahead of us and which gave us half an hour. We were beating into a five-knot wind. On the starboard tack we could come within one point of fetching—on port we sailed almost at right angles to the course. We and most other boats chose starboard tack without hesitation. We were pleased to see *White Mist* hold port tack until out of sight.

When we were let up a number of hours later and eventually fetched on a reach we were pleased with ourselves and might even have been sorry for *White Mist* if (1) we didn't think they had been stupid; (2) it was always fun to beat Blunt White (when we could). Imagine our surprise, upon finishing, to find *White Mist* had been in for 2½ hours!

While we had been "smart" doing the obvious, Blunt had been smarter (or luckier, said we) by tacking toward a line of clouds to the westward. Once there, he hit a strong new wind, tacked and reached in. It was many hours before said wind came down to us and let us fetch. *White Mist*'s chance of

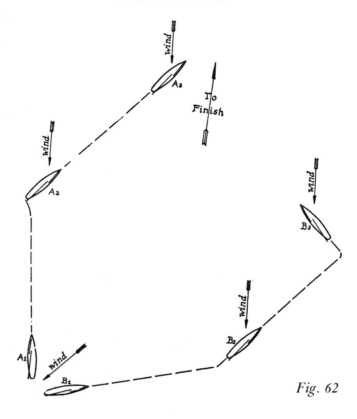

Fig. 62

winning (she got second in C and fourth overall to our seventh in C and eleventh overall) was spoiled because Dick Nye's *Carina* had been smarter still, heading west even earlier.

Keep Your Boat Moving

When on a dead beat in a distance race it's common sense to sail as hard on the wind, just as you would in an afternoon race, with just enough of a rap full to keep up speed against the higher seas. Whenever you're within a point of fetching a mark which is, say, 100 miles or so away, drive off harder if you can thereby pick up more speed. By bearing off 5° to 10°, you may pick up quite an edge in speed. If the wind holds exactly the same all the way to the finish, you will lose to the boat which worked to best advantage to windward. If the wind shifts, however, *in either direction* you will surely gain. And how seldom, except in the trades, does a wind hold true for a day or more at a time? If the wind heads you after a while you could then tack and cross the boats which had been holding high.

If let up, the boat which has been driving off may well fetch and the others overstand. About the only way you can lose by driving off is to have the wind hold absolutely steady or let you up very late when you're nearly abreast of the finish and about to tack. This risk is well worth taking. On some Bermuda Races I've seen boats strapped hard on the wind, going slowly, striving to keep on or above the rhumb line with over 600 miles to go, while others romped along just below it. Six hours later, on two occasions, the wind has hauled, letting the leeward boats reach up on a fast course.

Under such conditions the main consideration is speed, not course. "The course is six knots, approximately 150°" is the right instruction from the relieved helmsman.

What Course Down Wind?

It's often assumed that on a down-wind leg of a long race the preferred course is directly for the finish, or for the position a couple of hundred miles

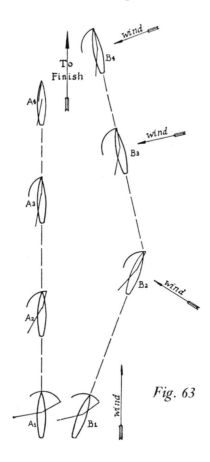

Fig. 63

ahead that you expect to find the best wind or most favorable current. Sometimes, of course, that is the way to go—many times it is not. Assume, for example, you are on a beam reach in fresh wind and expect the wind to fair. In this case sail low, perhaps even with spinnaker. Then when the wind does fair you will be able to sharpen up, maintaining a faster point of sailing than the high boats, which will be forced to run. This tactic is especially effective if you expect the wind to lighten. If you expect it to increase, it's usually better to hold a bit high in the early lighter stages to keep speed up. Then when the wind increases you can drive off at speed.

The old axiom of "up in the light stuff and off in the heavy" works even better on ocean races than in short ones. Of course, none of these tactics should be overdone because if they are you sail too much extra distance, and if conditions change just opposite to what you've expected you've really had it.

On a run, it's particularly suicidal to set a compass course for the finish. Hold high to keep the spinnaker full and to increase your apparent wind. If

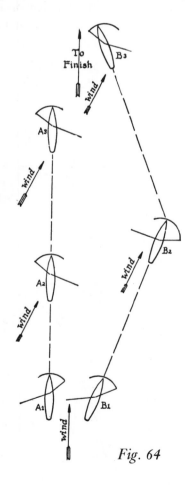

Fig. 64

you get headed you can get back down to a course for the finish. If freed you can jibe. See Figs. 63 and 64. In this distance, even if the wind stays exactly true for days on end, you won't have lost, and probably will have gained by tacking down wind. Yet sailing a compass course at sacrifice of boat speed is the most common error by the inexperienced distance racers. The idea is to keep speed on to get nearer the finish, *not* to crawl along a predetermined shortest line to the finish.

Avoid "Rhumblinitis"

This seems a good time to warn about "rhumblinitis" This is a common disease of drawing a line from start to finish, finding yourself off to one side of it and then clawing back to it "in order to sail the shortest rhumb line course." In any distance race the only rhumb line which makes sense is the line from where you are at the moment to the finish. Draw the original rhumb line to give a reference line but then don't worry about it unless the original rhumb line passes through the most favorable current area. Unless there's some such reason to claw back to the rhumb line, don't do it! This advice almost seems too basic but having a rhumb line fixation is a common error.

To Cover or Not?

Early in the race, don't worry about covering feared competitors. If you like where they are going, go there too. If not, let them go. You will never be able to cover them all the way anyway, and if you're right and they are wrong, by letting them go you have a real break. Never waste time pinching up to keep a slightly faster boat from passing to windward. This just slows both of you down while the rest of the fleet goes merrily on. Sail your own boat.

Near the finish, of course, if you have a narrow lead by all means cover a boat in sight which you know you have to beat. If slightly behind near the finish and being covered, you've got to take a chance and split. This is apt to be easier in a distance race than a short one, as night may come on and make it hard for a boat to cover.

In any event, in a distance race never give up, never stop thinking, never stop trying for that extra 100 yards per hour. *Finisterre* was not winning the 1960 Bermuda Race 100 miles from the finish (though she was doing mighty well). Then came the storm which upset many an apple cart, and she romped home. In one Stamford-Vineyard Race when I was sailing with Harvey Conover, we were half a mile behind *Mustang* with two miles to go. She gave us half an hour and we were both reaching for the finish in a moderate breeze. We thought that time we had him for sure, but Rod Stephens, as ever, never gave up. When the wind lightened and he sneaked past the Cows buoy just before a strong head current set in, he was home free while we had to anchor. He beat us by two hours!

It's the ever-changing conditions which make distance racing such fun. Sound tactics and perseverance are far more potent factors than luck, boat speed, or in my opinion, more important even than smart sail handling in determining the winner.

XVI

Racing at Night

HAVE YOU ever heard during the gams which follow every long or middle distance race how the winning boat, after failing to gain in daylight, drew ahead during the hours of darkness? Sure you have, because it happens all the time. And it is seldom because of luck that this happens. Luck does play a bit larger part at night but far more often the boats which gain then fully deserve to. How do they do it? There is no quick explanation, but rather a number of them which taken together should add up to more successful night racing. And since many long or middle distance races are won at night, the solution seems worth seeking.

Tactics remain pretty much the same, though there are a few changes which we shall discuss later. A larger factor in successful night racing is the ability to keep the boat sailing fast. The most obvious and best way to do this is to have as many really good helmsmen on board as you can. Have at least one top notcher for each watch, though two or more per watch is preferable. When sailing to windward at night, only the better helmsman should be at the wheel or tiller. If there is only one good one on each watch, he will lose his keenness if he tries to keep the tiller for all of the four-hour trick. He would be better off to take a half hour rest in the middle, checking on his relief as required.

With two or more good helmsmen on each watch, regular rotation is preferred. In some yachts, helmsmen change every half hour. This has the advantage of keeping them always alert. It has one possible disadvantage in that even a good helmsman sometimes takes a few minutes to gain the feel of the boat and to get in the groove. For this reason, one hour or longer tricks are preferred by many, though it seems to me that one hour should be the longest whenever there is more than one good helmsman.

Have the Right Equipment

Let's assume that we have set up the most efficient watch system we can devise for our particular crew but that even so we are a bit short on good

171

helmsmen. Since they don't grow on trees, this is a common problem. Our main concern then is how to become a better night helmsman and how to make night sailing easier. The first step is to equip your boat properly. The following will prove invaluable: (1) plenty of waterproof flashlights with good bright beams; (2) a light-colored masthead fly, or an electronic wind indicator; (3) white ribbon telltales on the shrouds and backstays; (4) a speedometer with a dimly lighted face (preferably a red light to prevent night blinding); (5) a lighted compass with a rheostat to adjust its brilliance.

In addition to the above minimum equipment, some skippers lash a flashlight in such a position that it shines up the luff of the jib (or the luff of the main if you prefer to sail by the mainsail). Such a light should not be brilliant since a bright, blinding light makes it difficult to see anything which is not lighted. With a light on the luff, one can spot the first quiver and keep the boat always on edge and going her best.

Disadvantages of steady lights on the sails are twofold. They make it difficult for you to see anything else because of the night blinding effect and they disclose your position to competitors. For these reasons, most skippers prefer to rely on a masthead fly and telltales, or an electronic apparent wind indicator, and only occasional use of flashlights on the sails; though some of the very best night sailors I know of keep a light shining continuously on the jib.

Sailing to Windward at Night

So much for equipment. How does the successful helmsman make use of it when sailing to windward? With a lighted jib, he will rely almost entirely on that, keeping it full but right on the verge of a luff. Whether or not his jib is lighted, he will refer frequently to the masthead fly (which should be lighted either permanently or when desired by a doorbell type push button in reach of the helmsman) or to shroud and backstay telltales. These will tell him if he is way off course and, if one uses them enough, to within a few degrees whether he is too high or too low. Flies and telltales are particularly useful in telling when one is too low. The jib will not luff when too low and, since the boat will often be going quite fast under such conditions, the angle of the masthead fly is the best safeguard against sailing lower than need be. The fly should stream approximately in the same direction as the main boom (actually a bit more to leeward). Any variation from this most efficient angle (which can best be ascertained by daytime checks) shows that the yacht is not on course. Should the fly stream more off to leeward, making a larger angle with the fore and aft line of your boat, you are sailing too low.

It should be easier to tell when one is sailing too high at night, but for beginners this is the most common fault. A light on the jib is excellent for showing when one is too high and so is the speedometer. If sailing too close to the wind, speed will drop appreciably. Since one gets a greater sensation of speed at night than during the day, it may be hard to sense when you have slowed down. When you first take the helm, experiment with the course to see what maximum speed you can get. This maximum speed is usually achieved when sailing a bit too broad for making the greatest gain to windward. So you may have to head a *bit* higher, even at some sacrifice in speed through the water. But as soon as the gauge shows you more than slightly below this top speed you know, unless the wind has dropped or the sea increased, that you are sailing too high.

Least helpful for efficient night sailing to windward is the compass. Some helmsmen sail to windward primarily on the compass, changing their course only after noticing a header or a let up. This is going about it backward. Too great attention to the compass is bound to make one slow to notice wind shifts with the result that one will be too high or too low much of the time. On windward legs, the compass should be used only as an occasional check, never to sail by. Checking it from time to time will show if you have been headed enough to warrant tacking and will also safeguard against being way off course without knowing it. But since the wind keeps shifting almost continuously, anyone who relies mostly on the compass will always be slow on the trigger. It is important, however, for each helmsman to refer to the compass often enough to determine what course he has made good on his trick. This course should then be entered in the log book so that the navigator can maintain a good dead reckoning position and so that the skipper or watch captain can decide when is the proper time to tack.

While all of these mechanical aids will prove helpful, a good helmsman relies most of all on "feel"—the ability to sense when the boat is going her best. You have doubtless heard much about how a top helmsman, by gripping the tiller lightly, can feel when the boat is going right. This ability is badly exaggerated. What one feels through a tiller is helpful but less so than other sensations which tell when the boat is "on." If such were not the case, one could not steer well with a worm gear wheel, yet many top helmsmen prefer such a wheel and have no trouble sensing when their boat is in the groove. The angle of heel, the action of the hull through the waves, the sensation of speed, the wind on his face (or the back of his neck)—these combine to tell a top helmsman when he is getting the most out of the boat. He feels more through the seat of his pants than through the tiller; he may be unable to explain just what tells him whether the boat is right or not, but he *knows*. A good helmsman lying in his bunk below can often tell when a poor one is not getting the most out of the boat.

To sum up, the formula for more successful night sailing to windward (using whatever helmsmen you may already have) is about as follows: Your boat is high when (a) the lighted jib or mainsail lifts or luffs unduly; (b) the speedometer shows an abnormal drop in speed; (c) the angle of heed diminishes; (d) the boat feels logy. She is too low when (a) the masthead fly or telltales are trailing to leeward at a sharper angle; (b) the amount of heel increases; (c) the wind feels more on the side of your face when facing forward; (d) the seas are more abeam; (e) the boat generally "feels" off. The compass is used only to check after you have already concluded that you are too low or too high.

Sailing Down Wind

When sailing on a reach or run, the compass is relied on more regularly, but not exclusively. A good helmsman will glance at it every 10 seconds or so, unless he is steering by a star or a light, in which case the compass need be looked at only occasionally. The rest of the time, he looks at the sails, the masthead fly, shroud telltales and speedometer. When he sees a slight header, he bears off; when freed, he sharpens up above the course. If the wind shift is more than a few degrees, or if it appears to be permanent, sails should be trimmed to correct for the new slant. In light spots, the helmsman will also order a trim so that he can head above the course and maintain best speed. In the puffs he will have sheets eased to get back below the course. In this manner, the rhumb line course is averaged and the boat kept moving at the best possible speed.

On reaches and runs, the crew is usually more active. If weather permits, one man should be stationed forward of the mast to warn when the jib or spinnaker (if on a close spinnaker reach) is breaking. To do this job, he will need a flashlight on dark nights, but nothing but good eyes on moonlit ones. Other crew members station themselves at the sheets, ready to trim to meet wind shifts or temporary changes in course. By working thus as a team, considerable ground can be gained. Crews who all sit in the cockpit may have fun shooting the breeze, but they don't win races.

Equipment for the Crew

We have already discussed how proper equipment can help the helmsman at night. The same holds true for the crew. Red glasses to be worn by anyone who goes below to check on the chart will keep him from losing his night vision. Without them, his eyes would not adjust as quickly to the darkness after returning on deck. When one crew member goes below to check the chart, he should close the companionway slide before turning on cabin lights. They should be out at all other times. Nothing blinds the helmsman more than cabin lights shining in his face. Life lines are a must for all boats which engage in extensive overnight racing. They not only may save a life, but permit the crew to work on deck with greater assurance and efficiency. For really rough weather, or for boats not equipped with life lines, have safety lines and safety belts for each man and see that they are hitched on whenever conditions warrant it. Also helpful are non-skid decks, either teak or one of the non-skid type paints. It goes without saying that every member of the crew should wear one of the better non-skid types of shoes and it should go without saying that crew members wear life jackets when working forward at night. This becomes especially important in rough weather.

The average yachtsman, however, is usually reluctant to wear a life jacket. Some of the more bulky types are a nuisance and make sail handling more difficult, but this is by no means the only reason why lifejackets are unpopular. To many sailors it seems "sissy" to wear a lifejacket. If you are a good swimmer this may be true during the day unless it is very rough. But at night if someone goes overboard there is not much chance of finding him until daylight. How many good swimmers can stay afloat an entire night? A few skippers have a standing rule that at night life jackets must be worn by all men outside of the cockpit. The pneumatic types or the "float coats" that provide flotation without bulk or discomfort should find favor with any shellback.

Some skippers paint the inside of the boat's rail white or some other light color, or even with a luminous paint. This warns the crew when they are near the rail and therefore lets them get about more quickly. Also helpful is white or luminous paint on the base of important deck fittings, permitting them to be located more easily and also to prevent tripping over them. Spreader lights are also of value. These are white lights set in reflectors on the under side of the spreaders. They should be aimed to shine directly down on deck. Most boats which have them may use them only occasionally because they blind the helmsman unmercifully. But when an accident occurs, when a hurried sail shift is required and when the spinnaker or other gear gets hopelessly fouled, spreader lights earn their keep. But except in these urgent cases, keep 'em out. The only real objection to spreader lights, in addition to their blinding effect, is the fact that they add weight and windage aloft. For this reason, some skippers prefer not to install them.

While the above will help the crew, of greater importance is what the crew does to help himself. Upon coming aboard in daylight, he should waste no time in orienting himself. Check and double check the position of all sheets, winches, cleats, etc. Check the halliards to be sure you could tell if blindfolded which is the spinnaker halliard, which the ballooner, jib or mainsail. And while you're checking this, make sure also that the spinnaker halliard is led clear and ready for hoisting. It is practically impossible to clear it at night. If racing on soundings, study the chart carefully and note the course. By having a thorough knowledge of the area and the lights to be seen, you won't have to check the chart as frequently, yet will still have a good notion of your position.

Night Racing Tactics

And now for a few thoughts on night racing tactics. For the most part, they remain the same as in the daytime, so we will consider only the changes. Darkness gives an opportunity to hide your movements, making covering more difficult. If being closely covered, it may be possible to break clear by showing no avoidable light for a while and then splitting tacks (it is against the rules, however, to turn off the red and greet sidelights or the stern light). This business of concealing your location is frequently overdone. If you have a real need for breaking clear (for example, if only a few miles from the finish and being closely covered by a boat ahead which you must pass to win) by all means avoid shining flashlights on your sails. It might pay to darken out if you don't want boats behind to follow you into what you consider a favorable position. But except in rare instances, it is far better to use all the lights you wish, relying more on speed than guile to gain the lead.

If racing along shore at night with an offshore wind, it often pays to sail close to the shore in order to remain in the night and early morning winds which more often than not are slightly stronger near the beach.

When beating to windward at night it is a strong temptation to tack as soon as headed. This may pan out during the day when you can see if you are really into a new slant and won't run right out of it if you tack. But at night it usually pays to keep going until well into the new slant and until convinced that it is reasonably permanent. Otherwise you run the risk of remaining on the edge of a new breeze without getting real benefit from it.

Lighthouses often seem closer at night than they really are. It is well, therefore, to take cross bearings to check position. I remember one night when we were running down on a lighthouse which had to be rounded before starting the beat home. The wind was light to moderate and there was a head tide. When we were within an estimated 200 yards of the light, we doused the spinnaker. This cut our speed so that we were barely able to breast the tide. After several minutes of making hardly any headway, we checked our distance from the light by a cross bearing and discovered that we were actually one third of a mile from it. We would have been there yet had we not rehoisted the spinnaker. While doing it two boats passed us, one of which went on to win the race.

It is important to allow more time for sail changing at night than during the day, but know your exact position so that you don't allow too much time.

Probably the most important factor for success in night racing is the enthusiasm of everyone on board. A crew which welcomes the darkness as a time for redoubled attention and effort to keep the boat going at her best and a helmsman who keeps trying every second of his trick, is a combination that's hard to beat. It is easy to put out during the daytime when you are wide awake and frequently able to see other boats and to tell if they are passing you, but it is another matter to stay on the ball when there is no one to compare your performance against, and when you are a bit sleepy to boot. The crew that does it, though, has its reward at dawn.

XVII

Match Racing Tactics

MATCH RACING is fun, exciting (especially at the start) and the lesson learned from it can be helpful in fleet-racing—and yet until 1964 in *Constellation* I had never sailed a match race. If you still haven't, you're missing plenty. You don't have to buy a 12-Meter to embark on match racing, since there are now many match race series. Some classes already sponsor match races and more seem destined to come. The N.A.Y.R.U. now conducts a North American match race championship for the Prince of Wales Trophy. Match racing minimizes luck, rewards daring and cool judgment and can, in closely matched boats, provide tremendous excitement.

All active racing men have engaged in match racing of sorts. Toward the end of a fleet race there is often just one boat left to beat. Even entering a series there may be one especially feared opponent which you might more or less match race. But for the best match racing excitement there should be just two boats from start to finish.

The most important time of a match race is the 10 minutes interval before the start. I say 10 minutes advisedly because five minutes is often too late to commence dueling with your opponent.

The key objective prior to the start is to get your boat directly on the tail of your opponent. If you can be directly astern and between a half to a full length distance, you are in the driver's seat.

To Get on the Tail

The advantages of this tailing position will be discussed but for the moment, please take my word that it is a good place to be, and let's explore how to get there and/or how to prevent the other boat from tailing you.

Often the element of surprise can be used as the boats approach each other in the starting area at approximately the warning gun, since one may not expect the other to start mixing things up. If your opponent seems to be slightly asleep at the switch you might be able to tack or jibe on to his stern before he is aware of what's up. To make this effective it is important for you and your crew to look relaxed and unconcerned and apparently paying little attention to the other boat.

In the last race of the 1964 Cup match we were able to surprise *Sovereign*. In the two preceding races we had stayed clear of *Sovereign* and avoided mixing it up prior to the start largely because we then knew our boat was considerably faster. By the last race Peter Scott seemed convinced that we were uninterested in playing the aggressor's role, and he was still checking the line, with his crew in relaxed mien at their stations, as we came sailing close by on a reciprocal course. It was a bit too tempting to resist, despite knowing that about the only way we could lose with a faster boat was to foul or be over the line early due to close maneuvering. I waited until Peter Scott, who had been looking at us, turned his gaze elsewhere apparently satisfied that we would leave him alone. At that instant we spun the wheel hard and tacked on to *Sovereign*'s stern before they realized what we were up to. Surprise won't work often against the same opponent, but it's worth a try.

A more effective way of getting the tailing position is through approaching the other boat on the right course and timing one's tack or jibe at precisely the right instant. If one can approach on a course which places you at least part way onto his tail rather than on the exact reciprocal, you've got an edge already. Fig. 65 shows two boats approaching on reciprocal courses and Figs. 66 and 67 show boat *A* approaching on a far more favorable course either to tack or jibe onto the other's stern. To get in these positions it is necessary to plan ahead. If the other boat is several minutes away from you and approaching, alter course either to windward or leeward, apparently for the purpose of passing at a considerable distance. Once you have gotten off to the side, assume a parallel reciprocal course and as you start coming closer together, gradually alter course toward the other boat, as shown in Fig. 68.

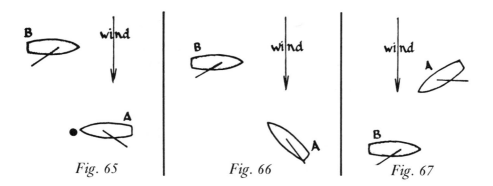

Fig. 65   *Fig. 66*   *Fig. 67*

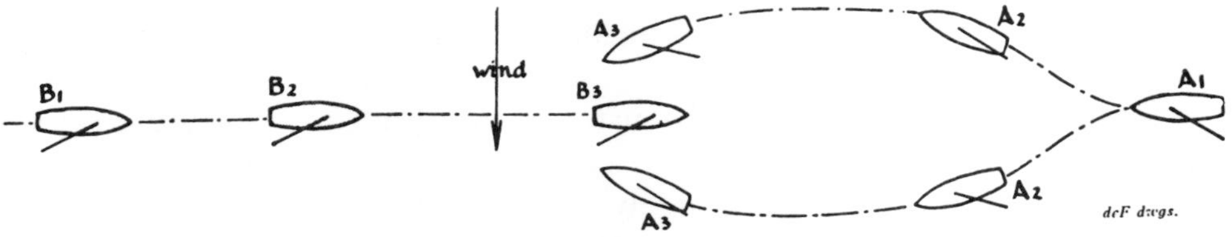

Fig. 68

The defense of boat *B* of course is to bear off or head up to keep on a reciprocal course and hence this tactic often fails. It is surprising, however, even in America's Cup competition, how often it does work provided one maneuvers with apparent indifference to the position of the other boat. At least it does no harm and may reap handsome dividends.

A more important consideration is to assume a course which will give you greater speed than the other boat. In light air, approaching on a close reach is preferred. In heavy air a broader reach is better. Proper maneuvering while still at a long distance from the other boat can get you onto the faster point of sailing. Keeping boat speed up is of prime importance because it permits you to swing more rapidly onto your opponent's stern.

The experts are divided as to whether it's better to approach the other boat from leeward or windward. Bill Cox of *American Eagle* preferred to approach from windward. Ted Hood of *Nefertiti* seemed to prefer to be to leeward so as to tack onto the other boat's stern. I was quite neutral, being happy either way *if* it gave greater boat speed.

In top competition it is unusual for one boat to get on the other's tail in the first pass, simply because the other guy is usually countering with the right move. What normally happens is that after one boat has tacked and the other jibed, they wind up still virtually parallel on reciprocal courses. If you are 15° to 20° closer to the tailing rather than the tailed position, you've done well. Even if you don't ever get on the other's tail (often the case) you are virtually assured that he won't get on yours—all that is necessary if your boat is even a bit faster, since it will almost assure clear air at the start if you time your moves correctly.

The timing, therefore, of your very first swing is vitally important. The basic rule is to be sure you start swinging soon enough. Start swinging *before* you come bow to bow. I can remember only once all summer when I started swinging too soon, and many times when I lost the initiative by swinging too late.

Once the first swing has been made it is usually followed by the typical ring-around-the-rosey pattern of both boats circling continuously hoping to get in a true tailing position. During these tacks and jibes the key requirement is to keep more boat speed on than your opponent. Applying too much rudder in an effort to spin faster can have an adverse effect, since it is apt to slow you down so that an opponent sailing wider circles at higher speed will complete his circle faster. After tacking, *don't* keep the rudder hard over in hopes of jibing faster. Instead, ease the helm so your boat can gain speed on a reach and only after speed is built up, following the tack, re-apply a sharp rudder angle to jibe swiftly. As the boat swings off, the crew must ease main smartly, both to keep speed on and also to permit bearing off faster. As soon as the jibe is completed the main must be trimmed swiftly to permit getting onto a close reach promptly, and finally, hard on the wind, prior to tacking.

It is vital that the jib be trimmed for best speed. Only possible exception is when tacking. Some skippers prefer to back the jib to help swing the bow over. On *Constellation* we were a bit leery of this since it seemed to kill boat speed unduly. We did, however, employ a slightly delayed castoff, just the beginning of backing, prior to letting the jib fly over.

This constant trimming, easing and then trimming of sails in circle after circle before the start is much the most exhausting time the crew will experience—far worse than a short tacking duel. It was vitally important, however. Even though our superbly conditioned crew on *Constellation* was about ready to drop after some seven minutes of this sort of drill, they never complained (seriously, that is), and always managed to get through that last circle before our final approach to the line. Then, when spectators thought they were dropping to the deck to reduce windage (partly true) they actually were dropping from being in a state of near-collapse.

Advantages of Tailing

There are several advantages to being in the tailing position. The greatest possible advantage is the possibility of keeping the other boat from tacking or jibing. If you are, say, half a length behind the other boat and can stay there, you might be able to drive her away from the line. This is particularly true if you can assume this position while on starboard tack because then if the boat ahead tacks or jibes into port tack you will have right of way. It can work also if on port tack, since a boat while tacking or jibing has no rights and the boat ahead must be careful not to tack or jibe too close to the boat astern. As the leading boat heads up to tack, the boat astern should go up too in hopes of blocking. If the boat ahead bears off to jibe, the boat astern should bear off and assume a course to block completion of the jibe. This is not balking, because the boat ahead is not maneuvering for the purpose of keeping clear

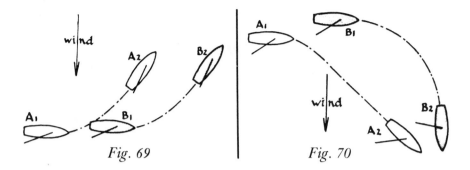

but rather for the purpose of getting back to the line, and there is nothing in the rules which says you must let her back. Once the jibe or tack is completed by the leading boat, then the tailing boat would be balking if she altered course to cause a collision, but earlier maneuvering to block the tack or jibe is OK. See Figs. 69 and 70 for tailing procedures to keep the leading boat from tacking or jibing. To be able to effect this, proximity to the boat ahead must be closely maintained, because otherwise she would have room to tack to jibe without fouling.

Even if unable to block the leading boat from tacking or jibing, which would make her late for the line, the tailing position has very real advantages. It gives more freedom of action since there is no possibility of the other boat blocking your approach to the line. You can break off the tailing process at the time of your choice and go for the end of the line you desire at the time you think best. If the boat ahead is far enough away to tack or jibe, you still have the advantage of being able to tack or jibe inside of her and possibly hamper her approach to the line. Or if she jibes or tacks early for the line, you can then let her go and head for the line later with full headway.

Where to Maneuver

The choice of where to initiate a tailing attempt depends on whether you believe your boat is faster. If you consider you are faster your primary aim will be to insure that you won't be blocked from the line and will have clear air at the start. If you consider you are slower, then aggressive tactics to block the other boat are worth the risk that the other might possibly block you.

The fast boat, therefore, should not initiate the ring-around-the-rosey procedure any earlier than necessary since the longer circling is continued the more chance one boat has of blocking or fouling the other. The fast boat will also want to do this maneuvering between the two ends of the line and well to leeward of it. Then even if the other gets on your tail, it is virtually impossible for her to shove you the wrong side of the starting mark, virtually impossible for her to keep you from approaching the line. All you need do is get enough gap to tack for the line early and then kill way until it's time to gain headway to reach the line on time.

Fig. 71 shows what can happen if you get tailed when beyond the extremity of the line. Here boat *B* is far enough ahead to tack but boat *A* can tack inside her and keep her from bearing off. In this position boat *A* can hold *B* off until it is time for *A* to go for the line. If *B* increases speed to attempt to pass to windward, *A* can go with her, forcing *B* to windward of the line. When time has run out *A* can get back to the line faster. It matters not at all that she is late, provided she starts sooner than *B*.

If you consider your boat slower than the opposition, then aggressive tactics are called for. Try to hook up with the other boat beyond the line extremities in hopes of being able to block her. Try to get on her tail early, even though this means you might wind up being tailed during the long period of circling. And, in particular, unlike the fast boat, don't break off tailing when you see you have an opportunity to reach the line with clear air. Instead of settling for that, keep in close contact with the other boat, try to either blanket her on her approach to the line or shove her over prematurely.

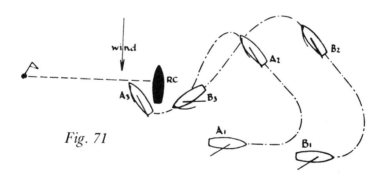

The Defense Once Tailed

If your opponent gets on your tail all is far from lost. Keep trying to shake her by better maneuvering while circling. This will usually not work since to get on your stern in the first place she must have been pretty fair at maneuvering.

If you can't shake her, try either reducing speed to make her overrun you or try increasing speed to open a sufficient gap to permit you to tack or jibe without fouling.

Reducing speed can be accomplished by lots of rudder action, by luffing sails, by going head to wind or by heading downwind with all sails trimmed flat, usually a combination of several of these. Above all do *something*, almost anything—don't let her drive you further and further from the line. By constant maneuvering and changes in trim you are apt to get free because it is difficult for the tailing boat to match your speed exactly. Incidentally, I have found that headway can be killed downwind more effectively by trimming the jib flat rather than letting it luff. If headway is killed enough to force the tailing boat to overlap, you then can jibe if she overlaps to windward or can tack if the overlap is to leeward.

One method of getting a sufficient gap to tack or jibe is to go hard on the wind in order to backwind or blanket the other boat. It is risky to continue this up to windward of the line, however, because the boat astern might be able to keep you from getting back down. See Fig. 72. This is a strong reason to start your maneuvering well below the line, unless you have a slower boat and want to be aggressive.

If you are tailed and maneuvering to leeward of the line and have room to tack or jibe, be sure to tack or jibe for the line a bit early. Then if the tailing boat turns inside of you she may be over the line early and even though not early, will have to kill headway so much that you might blast through her. If the tailing boat tacks or jibes for the line after you, you will be able to zigzag or kill headway enough to keep from being early at the line and may be able to blanket the boat astern. If the tailed boat were to tack for the line just on time the other would be able to turn inside and blanket enough to make her late.

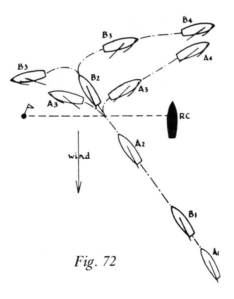

Fig. 72

This happened to me in the third Cup Race when I went for the line too late and *Sovereign*, which had been following us, jibed inside us and blanketed us as we approached the line. We did clear our wind by tacking to cross the line on our port tack but our heading back for the line too late did let *Sovereign* get a jump on us.

During pre-start maneuvers the tailed boat has an important refuge if she is able to head for the committee boat. She can then tack or jibe around the committee boat even though closely pursued because the tailing boats cannot cut the corner to block her from doing so. It is for this reason that one often sees in match racing the two boats circling tightly around the committee boat. When doing this, keep track of the time it takes to complete a circle and break it off when there is time to run down the line without being early at the leeward end. The tailing boat must then drop back either by making a wider circle or by killing way in order to get sufficient gap to avoid being back-winded.

In these circles the tailing boat should not always follow blindly. If the gap is enough she might be able to foil the boat ahead by suddenly going the other side of the committee boat and hence preventing her from tacking and driving her away from the refuge of the committee boat, as shown in Fig. 73.

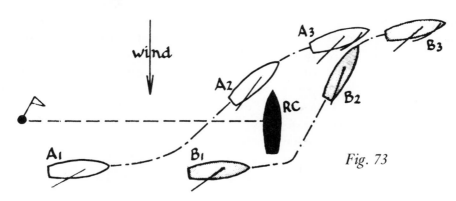

Fig. 73

If the boat ahead, however, is alert she can often foil such a maneuver by recognizing it early and taking different action just as soon as the tailing boat is committed to the other side of the committee boat. We fouled up *American Eagle* in just this way during the final trials. She was on our tail and we were reaching for dear life for the committee boat. Just as we passed to leeward of it and started swinging up to tack, Bill Cox, instead of following in our wake, went hard on the wind, as shown in Fig. 74, with the probable intention of either blocking our tack or tacking to leeward of us and keeping us from getting back down to the line. Since we had half expected him to do this we were ready and as soon as *Eagle* was committed to going to windward of the

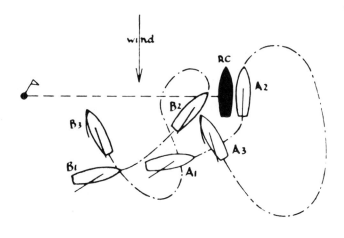

Fig. 74

committee boat, we abandoned our tack, bore off again on port tack and made
a wide swing back for the line, unhampered by our earlier tormentor. This
particular incident shows how quickly the fortunes can change for the two
boats and why it pays to be aggressive if your boat is a bit slow and why
conservative tactics are always prudent and wise for the fast boat.

It also shows the exciting developments which can accompany a match
race start. We have merely scratched the surface of the various situations
which can develop. This variety, the quick change in fortunes which often
occurs and the importance of the start in a two-boat race give match racing a
flavor and an excitement which is truly unique.

Once the start has been made the advantage is certainly with the boat on
top, but only if she makes the proper moves. Match race tactics after the start
are a lot more complex than merely covering the other boat.

Match Race Tactics After the Start

The popular conception that match racing after the start amounts merely
to covering if ahead and splitting if behind is pretty far from the truth. There
is much more to it.

It is true that if you are fortunate enough to be right on top of your
opponent at the start you should do everything possible to blanket him and
drive him further behind. The current rules which permit a boat to bear off
on the windward leg on a boat attempting to pass to leeward are a big help to

the leading boat. If the boat astern starts short tacking, match him tack for tack, trying always to keep him in your blanketed zone. So long as he is there, tack to cover even if you've got little headway on the present tack. He will too, and if you keep him blanketed it is mighty hard for him to gather headway on the new tack.

It's almost inevitable, however, that eventually the boat astern will get clear air. Once he has, it is often better not to match tacks exactly. If you see him tacking with little headway, but onto a tack which will give him clear air, it's usually better to wait until you have full headway before covering. You will surely gain distance by waiting, particularly if sailing a heavy displacement boat.

Once far enough ahead so that your blanket zone will not affect the boat astern, it becomes even more important to reduce the number of tacks. Each tack made heightens the chance of a foul-up on your jib sheet, increases the opportunity for other gear failure. Wait until the boat astern is about to cross your stern. Then tack and wait again until she is about to cross your stern on the next tack before covering, rather than always staying dead upwind.

An alert eye for wind shifts and a knowledge of which way the wind will tend is also vital in such a situation. If you expect a shift, favor the side where you expect the header. Let the other boat cross your stern when she is heading toward what you consider the unfavorable side of the course. Then when she is heading toward the favord side tack much sooner to cover, say dead upwind or even sooner. See Fig. 75, in which A allows B to be abeam on the un-favored tack. In this way you can encourage the boat astern to go the "wrong" way. If you are right in your judgment you can usually gain considerably. But don't be so sure of yourself that you let the other boat go entirely. This is the unpardonable sin in match racing, if carried to extremes.

If ahead and nearing the lay line, be sure not to overstand. Keep between the boat astern and the mark rather than dead upwind of her and don't hesitate to head for the mark just as soon as you think you have any chance of fetching. If you get lifted you may fetch, if headed you will have gained further. See Fig. 76. Usually if you do tack a bit early for the mark the boat astern will be sucked into overstanding because she is so thankful to have an opportunity to split with you. Another time not to cover is if you are nearly but not quite fetching and your opponent is either in your wake or dead to leeward and splits tacks. By letting her go then you will save two tacks and either a subsequent lift enabling you to fetch or a header will benefit you still further. Be sure, of course, that there isn't a stronger wind that your opponent is tacking into. If you suspect there is, then continue to cover.

Another time it is unwise to tack to cover is just as you enter a flat spot. By not tacking, the headway you enter the flat spot with will generate sufficient apparent wind strength to keep you moving at good speed for a long time

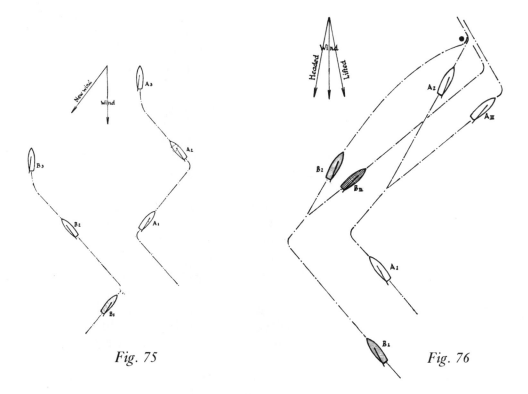

Fig. 75   Fig. 76

through the lighter air. If you were to tack instead, you would lose considerable headway in the process and then would have insufficient apparent wind strength to regain headway in the lighter local wind.

I learned this lesson the hard way in the second final trial race in *Constellation* against *American Eagle*. We were about five lengths ahead of *Eagle* and were applying a loose cover since we were going a trifle faster. Just after crossing *Eagle*'s bow on port tack we ran into a hole where the wind had dropped from seven to eight knots all the way down to three or four. Nevertheless, we tacked when almost dead to windward of her, dropping in speed from 7½ to 4½ knots in the process. With only a four-knot wind to help us on the new tack, we were unable to increase speed after tacking. Meanwhile, *Eagle* entered the flat spot dead to leeward of us but traveling at over seven knots. The increased apparent wind her headway gave her enabled her to blast on through and out ahead. By the time we emerged from the hole and had again built up headway *Eagle* had us and it took us literally 20 miles before we caught her, a mile from the finish.

Another time it is frequently unwise to tack to cover when ahead is when you have just entered a lift in a breeze which has been shifting back and forth. If you tack then you will tack into a header while the boat astern will surely tack as soon as you do but into the lift you have just left. She is sure to gain. If on the other hand you don't tack to cover, you will force the boat astern to continue sailing into a header. If the lift continues, you will have to tack to cover eventually (because it might continue to lift even more and put you on the outside of the circle).

At the outset of this chapter we assumed the boat ahead was blanketing or nearly blanketing the other at the start and advocated that she camp all over her luckless opponent. Let's assume, however, that while you are ahead at the start you are not blanketing the boat astern and can't blanket her quickly by driving off. If you are the faster boat, then it pays to keep sailing on the original tack just as long as the boat astern does. And even if you are no faster, or even if you think you are slower but feel the original tack is heading you toward the right part of the course, then keep sailing with the other boat since you already have the initial jump on her. But suppose you believe you are slower and further believe that the tack your pursuer is on is a poor tack. Here's the chance to startle the spectators and your opponent too by splitting with the boat astern. By so doing, you will be first into the area of the course where you expect to find a favoring slant or stronger wind. Your opponent will continue awhile in order to get well clear of you and then will probably tack over with you. If you were right in judging the favored part of the course you might well increase a one length lead tenfold and this will probably be sufficient margin to let you get on top of your faster opponent and hold him back. Had you not split when ahead, he probably, with wind clear, could have erased the small lead you had at the start. It takes courage to do this because if it backfires, reporters, spectators and even your own crew will think you were a fat dope not to obey "the cardinal match racing rule of covering when ahead." Never mind. If you are not a fat dope after all, and do have a good wind sense, this tactic is going to work most of the time.

Thus far we have been discussing what to do if you are ahead after the start. Alas, such is not always the case. If behind and blanketed, the first thing to do is get clear air and get it fast while still close. Bear off drastically, or tack the very instant you can after crossing the line. If blanketed on one tack, there's a good chance you won't be on the other. If despite driving off or tacking you are still blanketed, tack in quick succession, the second and third tacks coming almost as soon as you have steerageway. The boat ahead is apt either not to be able to tack quite as soon because she was not expecting you to tack at such short intervals or she is apt to wait on purpose in order to gain by not tacking with so little headway. True, she *will* gain, but you will have your wind clear. See Fig. 77.

Once your wind is clear and a series of sudden tacks has gotten you on a tack opposite to that of your opponent, what you do next depends on whether you think you are faster or slower. If faster, then try maintaining the tack

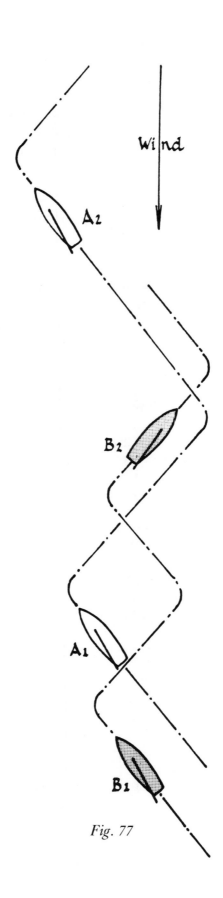

Fig. 77

which you get your wind clear on even after the boat ahead has gained headway and tacked to cover you. If you think you are slower or equal in speed, and particularly if you don't like the direction your clear tack is taking you on, then tack once again just as soon as your opponent tacks to cover you. If you always do this you will continue out of phase and will always be on a tack different from your opponent. She will be unable to blanket you and anything can happen in a furious tacking duel. A tacking duel with both boats always on the same tack is usually curtains for the one astern because she will be blanketed on at least one tack. But a tacking duel when carried on out of phase with each other equalizes matters.

In a tacking duel it is especially important, in your excitement to either break clear or stay on top, not to swing the boat too swiftly. Particularly in 12-Meters, and any heavy displacement boat, it pays to apply very little rudder and to come about in a long sweeping, even deliberate curve. By so doing you will shoot to windward in the process and you will not lose any more headway because a sudden tack kills headway, too. What's more, you will allow the jib trimmers extra time so that the jib will be sheeted home the instant you fall off on the new tack. It is particularly hard for the skipper of the leading boat not to hurry his tacks because psychologically he wants to be sure of covering precisely. This is a very real advantage to the trailing skipper unless the one ahead is extremely experienced.

We were amused in *Constellation* to read in the papers how one or more of our opponents had showed great prowess in tacking in nine seconds as opposed to our 11 or 12. The winches and in particular the crew of *Constellation* were second to absolutely none when it came to getting that jib around and sheeted home. If anyone tacked faster it was because we didn't want to tack faster than we did. In the second trial race against *Eagle*, 80 tacks were made. In the first leg when we were ahead, we were tacking as fast or faster than *Eagle* in my anxiety to camp on her. In the last leg when 40 tacks were taken in quick succession, she was "out tacking" us. Only rub for them was that *Constellation* went by with her more deliberate tacks.

The one thing the trailing boat must concentrate on above all else is to stay close and not take fliers. Don't try to split with the boat ahead just for the sake of splitting. If she lets you go it is almost certain that you are going the wrong way. Even when behind, just so long as your wind is clear keep going what you consider to be the right way. If thereby you can stay close, you've got leeward legs or later windward legs to pass on but an early flier can get you in a position from which you can't recover.

Be careful in your anxiety to get clear, not to overstand, and avoid, if possible, taking any more tacks than the boat ahead. Patience was never more of a virtue than in yacht racing. Just keep plugging along, using your head not your emotions to guide you, and there's a good chance that boat ahead will make a slip you can capitalize on.

If you see a flat spot up ahead and will soon want to tack, tack before reaching the flat spot, especially if the boat ahead is already in it. Remember our earlier discussion of losing apparent wind strength by tacking in such a lull.

If in a shifty breeze, tack as soon as you are headed. The boat ahead probably will have waited before tacking in a header, and hence on each header you have a great chance to close the gap. This, of course, is not true if it means tacking directly into his blanket zone but is certainly true if dead downwind of him but far enough away not to be affected by bad air.

If you, as trailer, have done your job well and have an even boat, you will be close on the leader's tail as he rounds the weather mark, and there another fascinating part of a match race begins.

If you round the windward mark first, start out on what you consider is the fastest course for the next mark, not necessarily the direct course. If going onto a run which will require tacking downwind and you have a fairly sizeable lead, go half the distance of your lead on one tack, then jibe over. In this way you will be directly between your opponent and the mark when she rounds. Don't worry about also being dead downwind. You won't be blanketed because you won't be running dead before it. Thereafter stay between your opponent and the mark, matching his jibes. It is not so effective covering to be dead ahead of the boat astern while tacking downwind. Stay instead on her leeward bow. If you don't, a sudden jibe by the boat astern will put her well up on your quarter and in a blanketing position. Keep a weather eye peeled for wind shifts or puffs and govern your course accordingly, and don't forget to go off in the puffs and up in the light spots. In short, while you will want to cover the boat astern don't get so preoccupied with her that you fail to sail your own to best advantage. I think it is because of this preoccupation that the trailing boat in a match race very often gets through. Don't be guilty on that score.

When on a reach, the leading boat has an opportunity to gain if she doesn't cover precisely. Frequently the boat astern will hold high or very low of the course in an effort to sail around you. If you think her course is excessively high or low don't match it. Instead go only part way in covering. There is nothing more discouraging for the boat astern which is holding high on a reach in hopes of putting you onto a run for the mark to see you staying down on a fast reaching course, covering only slightly. When the trailing boat finally bears off for the mark the leader is usually far gone. Of course the leader must be sure it's desperation and not favorable wind which is making the trailing boat sail off course. If the latter, then go with her.

If there's a question as to whether or not to carry spinnaker and you have a good lead, wait until you see what the trailing boat is doing before you set yours. And if there is real doubt, wait until well after hers is set. Take stadimeter readings and set your chute too only if they show she is gaining. The basic rule is for the leading boat to match the sails carried by the trailing one but always keep in mind that the boat astern may be trying something desperate. No need to hang yourself along with her.

If behind on a downwind leg the first consideration is to stay close and check how you are doing before splitting. If you think the boat ahead is sailing a good course *don't* sail a different one just for the sake of being different. In short, continue to sail your own race and see if you can't sail by, rather than around, the leader. If you see you aren't gaining, then a modest amount of splitting is in order, but don't overdo it. On a reach hold a bit high. If the boat ahead comes up with you go still higher. In this way you might well suck her up to make a run for the mark where you may be able to blanket her. But above all be careful not to go too far up unless the other boat comes with you. Don't try to go by with each manuever. Better by far to attempt to gain slightly with the hope of getting close enough to go by later when opportunity beckons.

On a run the trailing boat is often well advised to initiate a jibing duel. If you can jibe better you've got a great chance, and even if not, there is always the chance the boat ahead will muff a jibe. Besides, each time you cross her stern in such a duel you give her a momentary dose of disturbed air.

In a shifty wind, jibe just as you are lifted. If the boat ahead jibes at the same time she will have a poorer sailing angle until the lift gets down to her. In the meantime you will surely gain.

If you are behind on a reach don't set a spinnaker unless you are reasonably sure it is the right thing to do. If in doubt then it's worth trying a different sail combination than the leader. But don't do it just for the sake of being different.

On a run it's often desirable to set a reaching spinnaker in order to be more efficient in a jibing duel. In such a duel the yachts are hardly ever on a run and one with a running spinnaker up has a real handicap. If you are ahead and have a big lead set a running chute. If close ahead or behind it is safer to put up a reacher.

When all is said and done, the main consideration for both boats in a match race is to keep cool, keep doing the logical rather than being a slave to the dictum that "if ahead cover, if behind try to split." The boat astern has a psychological advantage and if she never gives up, always trys to gain a foot here and another there, she is very apt to wear the leader down. In any event, match racing in evenly matched boats is one of the most exciting forms of sailing. Try it and see.

XVIII

Anticipation

ANTICIPATION, in my opinion, is the key word to racing success. Any good sailor can steer a boat fast. All experienced racing men know basic tactics we have discussed in earlier chapters such as tacking on headers, staying (when ahead) between a boat and the finish and, while reaching, bearing off in puffs and heading up in the light stuff. And yet the same guys still keep on winning. What sets them apart? In my book, it is their greater ability to anticipate, to think ahead and plan ahead, to sail with more thought on what will or may happen later rather than what is happening.

By this I don't mean gambling all on a change in conditions which may or may not materialize, but rather being prepared so that if it does happen you will be ready for it and will benefit. It is not a form of anticipation to go off on a flyer, leaving the fleet on a windward leg in hopes of a wind shift which will put you on top. Unless there is almost unmistakable evidence that this will transpire (and the fact that the bulk of the fleet disagrees makes this unlikely to start with) this is gambling, not anticipating. If anticipation is used properly, one will not be hurt much, if at all, if it doesn't pan out but will benefit if it does.

Anticipation starts even before going on board. The good skipper thinks about what the conditions may be at race time. If he anticipates a heavy wind later, and doesn't have a steady crew, he lines up one on the heavy side—the reverse if he expects light air. Unless he is sure it's going to blow hard, however, he doesn't get an extremely heavy crew, nor does he get an extremely light one unless he is sure of light air. Rather, he gets one which will be adequate in any wind.

The same applies on choice of sails. He chooses a sail which he expects will be best for the average conditions during the race rather than conditions which prevail at the time of setting out. If practicable, he brings along a second suit in case he guessed wrong, so that a last-minute shift can be made.

The good skipper is never late getting out to the start, because he has anticipated that the wind might die or come ahead or that an expected tow might not materialize. He always leaves early.

The successful skipper never reads course signals incorrectly because he knows from bitter experience how easy it is to do so. I got my lesson the hard way by losing the Raven National Championship in just this fashion. We had a safe lead in the last race and the series apparently sewed up. I had read the course signal for the second mark as "O," hence dutifully rounded it and started up wind. The next five boats followed us but the sixth and eventually most of the fleet including the winner (who had been in 16th position) went right past and continued down wind.

A frenzied look at the circular showed us that there was a mark "Q" down there and it dawned on us too late that I had read "Q" as "O." In my rather prejudiced view the letter "Q" should never be used for a signal as it is all too easy on quick glance to miss that little tail to the letter, as half the Raven fleet did. I will make many errors in the future, will surely fail to anticipate things I should, but will never confuse "O" and "Q" again because I know that it is possible to so confuse them.

In choosing the right end of the line to start at, anticipation can be vital. Don't feel unlucky if you pick the favored end yet get a poor start because there is such a jam of boats trying to cross there that all but one or two are blanketed. A smart skipper will foresee this and will probably start near but not at the favored end, settling for a second-best start in order to avoid the jam.

In choosing which end to cross on, one should anticipate the conditions not just at the start but several minutes thereafter. For example, on a windward start if it is obvious that the favored tack after the start will be port, don't start to leeward even if it is definitely favored. If you get a perfect start to leeward you might be able to tack and cross the fleet. Anything less than perfect will mean that minutes will pass before you can go where you know is right, and the advantage of the line will be wiped out and then some. Under these conditions it's better to start to windward, even a late start there. Or, perhaps you have enough nerve to try a port tack start. This would be the time to do it.

On the northeastern coast of the United States, northerlies are traditionally puffy and with wide wind shifts. These shifts usually follow a pattern or phase. On one day the shifts may come at three-minute intervals, on another five, six, or seven minutes. It is amazing how regular the pattern is—not always but generally. It pays, before the start, to time the interval between shifts. If one determines that on a particular day the phases are at five-minute intervals, this can be of the greatest value.

Say, for example, that right at the five-minute gun a shift occurs which makes the windward end favored. This will entice many skippers to go for that end. The skipper who has established a pattern of the shifts will know that approximately at the start the wind will shift back. He starts to leeward, therefore, has little company there and about at gun-time gets a "lucky" shift which puts him nicely on top. It doesn't work out that way all the time, and seldom precisely on schedule, but it does work out with enough regularity so that under these conditions one should start in accordance with the wind phases for that day. There is no form of anticipation which gives more satisfaction—a satisfaction which is not lessened by everyone thinking you are lucky.

Anticipating shifts by knowing the phases for a given day can also be of great help throughout the windward leg.

Again considering the start, however, don't feel unlucky if you get over the line early on a strong fair current and light wind. An anticipating skipper will realize that if this happens so much time will be lost trying to get back that a poor race is inevitable. Hence, under these conditions, which usually cause several premature starters, the good skipper plays it safer than usual. He may be over early occasionally but never under conditions which make premature starts so very damaging. In a strong head tide and dying wind, anticipation takes the form of staying up tide and sometimes even the wrong side of the line before the start and having an anchor rigged and ready. If the wind poops at the gun you will be able to anchor right on the line and get off in the lead when the wind returns.

Once the race has started, anticipating changes in tidal effects can be of great help. This was brought home to us in most happy fashion in a Huntington Day Race on Long Island Sound. We had a beam reach from the start in Huntington Bay to a turning buoy out in Long Island Sound. While still in the Bay there was little tide effect but a look at the current charts showed we could expect a strong tide setting us to leeward once clear of the protecting shore. We also noticed as we reached toward the Sound that the wind ahead was gradually getting lighter. As a result we held high to get up tide before we hit into its full strength on our weather beam. When we did hit it, we kept sighting on the buoy and adjusting course to see that we were not being swept to leeward of it.

By the time the rest of the fleet realized the danger and tried to make ground up tide the wind had died still more. It hung on long enough for us to crab down to the mark from our weather berth, with the tide on our quarter actually helping us. The others, who saw their peril too late, were unable to keep from being swept to leeward of the mark and had to anchor. We coasted down tide and had rounded the *second* mark 4½ miles away before the breeze increased and let the next boat round the first mark.

Of course we had been very lucky indeed to have the wind drop as much as it did, but I don't feel our exaggerated course was a gamble. If the wind had held we still would have gotten tide advantage by being to windward. I omit any anecdotes of the times we have been caught down tide and realized our error too late, but believe me it's happened. When it happens again I'll not feel unlucky, but will realize that I could and should have anticipated it.

Anticipation of current effect takes other forms. When making a passage down a long bay such as Long Island Sound with a fair tide it is vital to anticipate where one might be when the current turns foul. I've been caught out in the middle just as the tide turned and the wind lightened and have had the bitter experience of watching boats inshore ease past and go out of sight ahead simply because they had, *while they were still able to*, gotten into the more moderate head current or back eddies near the beach.

Even without tide to consider it is important on reaching legs to anticipate the change in wind velocity. I don't mean just going off in puffs and up in light air, but attempting to forecast what the general trend will be. If, as you start a reaching leg, you anticipate a gradually strengthening wind it pays to average a course high of the rhumb line in the first part of the leg. This will give added speed through a more favorable sailing angle. Then when the wind does come up you will be able to drive down to the mark at good speed.

Just the reverse should be followed if one expects the wind to lighten—sail low of the course early in the leg and reach up at good speed in the lighter wind later on. This takes considerable courage because in the first part of the leg the boats which held high will usually draw ahead. If the wind does lighten it will be most rewarding, and even if the wind holds steady you will lose little or nothing unless you've overdone it.

This form of anticipation is most fruitful in distance races or long reaching legs. On the Stamford-Vineyard or Storm Trysail Club's Block Island Races, for example, the start is late in the afternoon and usually a nice southerly is blowing. Usually also, after the sun has set the wind starts abating. Many boats hold high during daylight hours, partly because in a long race it is hard to resist a course which will give more speed at the moment. Others hold high because there are times when after dark the wind holds stronger under the windward shore than out in the middle. Despite this latter consideration which *sometimes* gives the windward boats a distinct advantage, the winning course usually is to hold out in the middle until the wind starts to lighten and only then sharpen up and head to close the beach.

Unless there is much more wind under the beach, this will surely work out. It fails to work just often enough to make the race interesting and also often enough to encourage many boats to hold high early. It must always be remembered, however, that what goes up must come down, and unless the wind is stronger when the shore line forces them down the windward boats are sure to suffer, while those offshore reach up through their lee at a more favorable angle.

It is important to anticipate gear failures so that if they do occur little time is lost. For example, if the wind increases a great deal during a spinnaker run, the skipper who is thinking ahead will double up on the after guy. If your after guy parts and thus causes the loss of several minutes—or worse—don't feel unlucky. It all could have been avoided by having a second guy already rove in anticipation.

Failure to anticipate a gear failure cost us seven minutes in one Block Island Race. When half a mile from the island, the wind shifted from a reach to a dead beat and increased to 30 knots. We had our largest genoa on, a sail of lighter weight and larger size than the conditions called for. Since we had so little distance to go before rounding, I figured we would lose more by shifting to a smaller headsail than by lugging our large one. Then 200 yards from the turning buoy the big genoa split in two. With no other headsail bent on we almost stopped in our tracks. In a hurry to get a smaller jib on her, we tossed it on deck but, still in its bag, it slipped overboard before the foredeck crew could grab it. Since we needed that sail we jibed over and went back for it, all of which took time.

Had we lost the race by seven minutes or less I would have shot myself. I feel we were right in trying to get around the mark without shifting jibs but dead wrong in not anticipating the trouble we got into. It would have been so easy to bend on a smaller sail when the wind came ahead and increased, not to use unless necessary but to be ready just in case.

Anticipating the need for sail shifts can be important also when there is no chance of the sail blowing out. If beam reaching under spinnaker, one should anticipate the possibility that the wind may come ahead and be prepared by having a ballooner or genoa bent on. Then if it does come ahead suddenly little distance is lost in shifting. By the same token, have a spinnaker ready, rigged and willing before it can be used to advantage. If the wind fairs you can get a real jump by being first to crack on the new sail.

On the same line of reasoning, blame only yourself and not luck if your spinnaker wraps around the headstay and can be neither raised nor lowered. This can and does happen in a heavy sea and the good skipper will always have a spinnaker net rigged *before* it happens.

Time can also be lost if light weather sheets are not rigged and ready so that they can immediately replace heavy ones just as soon as they become more efficient, in lightening airs. Greater trouble comes with not having heavy sheets ready to replace light ones, if the wind increases suddenly.

In a small boat which has hiking straps, don't wait until you need them before rigging them. Rig 'em beforehand. If you don't need them you have lost nothing—if you do you will gain a lot over the guy who waits until the breeze pipes up and then has to keep the crew inside rigging hiking straps instead of using from the first moment they were needed.

On the Six-Meter *Goose*, sailing in the Gold Cup races, we lost lots of ground once by sticking with a single part mainsheet until *after* the breeze had piped up and the double part sheet was vital. It would have been simple to double up in light air but murder to do it in a strong blow. Racing Lightnings in the Mallory Cup finals at New Orleans we showed the same lack of anticipation as regards jib sheets. It was light at the start, so we made direct single-part leads to the jib sheets. We erred in not doubling them up prior to being hit by a squall. During the squall it was impossible to trim the jib effectively, and very damaging taking time to double them after the wind freshened and made the job much more difficult.

XIX

The Care of Sails

WHEN THE SCHOONER yacht *America*, racing in 1851 against the largest and fastest British yachts, beat the fleet and won the cup which for all time bears her name, she proved, among other things, the importance of well shaped sails for making a yacht go fast. The *America*'s sails were made of cotton, while the British yachts' sails were flax. The cotton sails retained their shape far better than the flax ones which were prone to bag and bulge in the wrong places.

Good, well shaped sails are every bit as important today. The best materials are available to you for your sails but to break them in properly and to keep them in good shape they must be cared for wisely and well.

Many years ago Ratsey & Lapthorn, Inc., sailmakers of City Island, N.Y., produced a booklet bearing the same name as the heading of this chapter. With their permission the greater part of it was quoted in earlier editions of this book because I felt it presumptuous to try to improve on it. In subsequent years, however, the advent of synthetic sails has so changed the picture that it is necessary to update their booklet which is now out of print. I am pleased, however, to be able to quote much of Ratsey's timeless advice on Battens, the Flow in Sails, Masthead Sheaves, Straight Lines, Sail Storage and Overhauling Sails.

Breaking in a New Sail

In the days of cotton sails, breaking in was extremely important and took many days. It was imperative not to hoist or haul out a new cotton mainsail too hard and to sail it only in dry moderate weather. With the advent of Dacron, some breaking in is still desirable. The common fault now is not hoisting or hauling out a new sail hard enough. It should be hoisted nearly (but not quite) as hard the first time as it ever will be. On a luff of 20 feet hoist to within a couple of inches of final tension. After several hours of sailing thus it can be hoisted to its final dimensions and can be sailed in strong winds and wet weather without damage.

200

It's important to remember, however, that every racing sail has just so many effective hours of life. While day sailing, therefore, it's wise to use an old sail, saving your best only for the race.

It's important also not to hoist sails until you're ready to cast off from the mooring. Shaking is not good for them or for their stitching.

In cotton sails it was imperative to dry them before bagging or furling in order to prevent mildew. While Dacron sails don't mildew to the point of losing strength, they do discolor slightly if bagged or furled wet and it makes me feel better anyway to dry them just as if they were cotton.

Avoid Overexposure to Sunlight

One thing synthetic sails, particularly nylon, don't like is too long exposure to sunlight, which makes the cloth lose strength. This isn't a serious problem since Dacron and nylon are so strong but it is wise when through sailing to keep the sails covered with sail covers or bagged.

Bag Sails with Care

Another precaution which is desirable, particularly in small boat Dacron sails, is to bag them with care. A small boat's sails are often heat set to such a degree that the cloth is very hard and stiff. If stuffed into a bag it develops wrinkles or cracks in the surface which will reduce speed and perhaps even shorten the sail's life. The sail will stand bagging for many years but this practice doesn't permit as smooth a surface and hence is bound to reduce speed at least to a slight degree. It is better, therefore, to roll a sail along the foot as it is lowered, eventually getting a long cylindrical shape. This cylinder is then coiled (not folded) into the bag. This takes a bit longer than stuffing but through the years will pay off. The same should be done with the jib, starting the roll from the bottom.

On larger boats it is more difficult to roll sails, but they should at least be flaked instead of stuffed into a bag. This is particularly important with mylar or kevlar sails, neither of which should *ever* be stuffed into a bag. To accommodate them sailmakers now supply long sausagelike bags with zippers running their full length. The sail can be rolled or flaked on deck, laid into the long bag and then zipped up. The less heading any sail gets, the smoother its surface and the longer its competitive life will be.

Small boat mains should always be removed after racing and rolled for storage. On larger boats they should be flaked or furled smoothly and kept on the boom. *Always* cover them with a sailcover, not so much for protection from rain or dew as to insure that they are not exposed to the damaging rays of the sun.

Slack Your Outhauls

In the days of cotton sails it was imperative to ease outhauls in wet weather or whenever the sails were lowered since rain, spray or dew would cause the foot rope to shrink more than the sail, and hence pull the sail out of shape. Dacron sails usually have Dacron bolt ropes quite impervious to shrinking, but it is still recommended to ease the outhaul whenever the sail is lowered.

Battens

The leech of your mainsail is usually cut with a convex edge, or "roach," as it is popularly called. Pockets for fiberglass or wooden battens are placed at intervals along this edge. Never hoist a sail without inserting the battens in their proper pockets. For if they are not used, the "roach" will not hold itself flat, and the weight of the boom will stretch the sail in a straight line from headboard to clew. But when the battens are in place, the whole roached area of the leech will take its share of the strain, and the sail will stretch evenly and naturally throughout the entire area.

Have your battens a bit shorter than the pockets in which they fit. If they are too long they will wear a hole in the inboard end of the batten pocket, or through the body of the sail itself.

The unroped leech of a sail will stretch practically all it is ever going to stretch the first time the sail is used. That is why, among other reasons, we recommend that luff and foot should be pulled to the "made length," to help stretch the whole sail evenly. If the luff is not set up to the "made length" the after end of the boom is apt to droop and swing too low, putting undue weight on the leech.

When hoisting sail, take the weight of the boom on the topping lift until the sail is hoisted all the way up—or, in a small boat, have someone hold the boom up. It is not fair treatment to make the sail take the weight of the boom until the halliard is set up and the luff taut.

The Flow in Sails

As almost all sailors know, the most effective form of a sail is one which, generally speaking, is curved in a similar manner to a bird's wind—the forward section of the sail has a distinct curve, or flow, which gradually flattens toward the middle of the sail, ending in a practically flat surface in the region of the leech, or after edge. It is not at all unlike the curve so carefully constructed in the wing of a modern airplane. The wing of an airplane, mounted "on end" in a small boat, has, in fact, been made to propel the boat to windward.

In a Marconi, or jib-headed, sail, the draft, or flow is kept in the forward part of the sail by setting up on the halliard or cunningham so that there is more strain on the luff rope than there is on the foot rope. It is important not to have the luff so long that it cannot be made really taut by hauling on the cunningham—a must for heavy-weather sailing.

If the foot is too long for the boom, the sail cannot be flattened out as much as we might wish, but it will not cause the draft to come too far back in the sail.

Masthead Sheaves

The lead of the main halliard as it leaves the mast on the after side should be vertical. This is accomplished by having a halliard sheave of larger diameter than the masthead and putting the pin of the sheave just abaft the center line of the mast. This results in the sheave protruding from the after end of the spar. If a smaller sheave is used, the halliard is sure to pull the headboard of the sail against the track. This will soon cause the seizing of the topmost mainsail slide to chafe off, and the track will chafe through the top part of the luff rope before long.

Most modern beats have luff grooves instead of tracks to accommodate the mainsail belt rope. Even so, a large diameter halliard sheave is important.

If a permanent backstay is fitted, a wooden or metal "crane" device should be attached to the after side of the mast above the sheave, and the stay set over this crane in order that it may not interfere with the headboard of the sail.

Straight Lines

When sighting along the foot of the sail, be sure that the gooseneck fitting, and the clew outhaul fitting, keep tack cringle and clew cringle in a straight line with the foot of the sail. Frequently they do not. Sometimes the gooseneck fitting is too high, rarely too low. In either case, the sail cannot set properly. The same is true of the clew. For instance, most sails, attached to a boom by the use of track and slides, or by means of a jackstay or lacing, will set for almost their entire length in a straight line an inch or so above the boom. Then suddenly, at either or both ends, there is an abrupt angle where the corners of the sail are attached. No sail should be expected to set properly under these circumstances. See that the fittings at both ends of the boom are such that clew and tack cringles are held in a straight line with the foot of the sail. Otherwise, wrinkles will develop, and become permanent if allowed to remain for any length of time.

Nowadays it is more common to have the foot of the main in a groove on the boom, doing away with slides. Be sure that the tack and clew cringles are positioned properly to induce a straight-line pull without distorting the sail.

Headsails

Headsails used to have wire luffs, but now almost all of them have stretchy luffs. Shape can be modified drastically by changing halliard tension, increasing it for heavy-weather sailing and decreasing it as the wind lightens.

If your jib is cut with a mitre seam, the angle at which the sheet pulls is most important. The mitre seam bisects the angle at the clew, and if an imaginary line is drawn from the deck lead through the clew of the sail, it should strike the stay above the mitre seam. This is true for most jibs and staysails. For Genoa jibs, of squarer shape, this line should usually strike just below the mitre seam. Owing to the multitude of shapes and sizes of jibs and staysails it is impossible to make any hard and fast rule—experience, and trial and error, are the best rules.

Get Off Your Boat

In order to determine the set of your sails, and the proper lead and trim of sheets, it is distinctly advisable to get aboard some other craft while someone else sails your boat around. You will see things which are in no way apparent when you are aboard your own craft. Take a good, long look, from all angles. You can, most certainly, see many things from your own cockpit. Nevertheless, "see your sails as others see them." Your time will be well spent.

Reefing

With the advent of jiffy reefing it is no longer difficult to tie in a reef, and easier still to shake it out. There are a few caveats to prevent damaging the sail. To reef, first lower the main halliard and place the luff cringle on the hook adjacent to the gooseneck. Next haul on the reefing line (with a winch, if necessary) to haul the leech cringle down to the boom. Then rehoist the halliard. For all intents and purposes the reef is now effective, except for the fact that there are folds of reefed sail flapping below the boom. Tie these up to the boom with good-sized reefing lines (sail stops work well) to get a smooth foot with all folds out of the way. It is vital to reverse the process when shaking out the reef. First cast off the reefing lines along the foot. If either the leech or luff reefing line is cast off first, the sail along the boom could be torn or pulled out of shape. Next cast off the reefing line at the clew, ease the halliard to get the luff cringle off the hook then hoist away.

Some boats are still equiped with roller reefing. Jiffy reefing is faster and retains the sail's shape better, but should you not wish to go to the expense of conversion, adequate reefs can be made by rolling. Be sure to have one crew member hauling on the leech as the sail is rolled in order to avoid wrinkles.

When through sailing, do not fail to shake out a reef just as soon as possible, especially if the sail is wet or damp. Leaving a sail reefed unnecessarily will stretch the sail along the row of reef points, and induce mildew.

Salt Spray

Particularly on small boats, and sometimes on large ones, sails become soaked with salt spray. Even when dry, sails of light material, impregnated with salt, will almost crackle like a piece of paper when handled. Again, when damp or foggy weather sets in, the salt in the sail quickly absorbs the moisture, and the sail is wet.

The remedy for salt-incrusted sails is to rinse them out thoroughly in fresh water. Small sails can be washed out in the bath tub. Larger sails can be "hosed down" with a garden hose on the front lawn. Or, you can send your sails to your sailmaker and have him rinse, scrub and clean them—a practice becoming more popular as yachtsmen become appreciative of it.

Sail Storage

When laying up your sails for the winter, be sure, first, that they are perfectly dry. Then, after removing the battens, fold them carefully, and store them in a clean, dry place.

Beware of "boat lockers." Not only are they apt to be damp if situated close to the water, but rats take a fiendish delight in devouring sails whenever they get a chance. Be sure, therefore, that your storage space is clean, dry—and ratproof.

Overhauling Sails

By the end of the yachting season the newest and best of sails may need an overhaul—seams and lashings may have become chafed, batten pockets ripped, and so on. Most yachtsmen store their sails away in a hurry, and wait till spring to inspect and make repairs. Our advice is to inspect and repair your sails before storing for the winter—then you are a lap ahead of the usual spring rush. And, if the repairs are of such a nature as to require the services of a sailmaker, ship your sails to him immediately—let him do the work in the "off" season, when he has plenty of time and little work—you may get a better job, and probably a lower price. At any rate, you will do the sailmaker a favor—and be sure of having your sails in apple pie order for next season, no matter how early that season starts.

XX

Sailing to Win

READERS WHO ARE still with me after nineteen chapters will agree that yacht racing is not a sport which can be mastered in a day. Observance of the principles outlined here should improve one's results. But they aren't all there is to winning a race.

The successful skipper must know the principles behind yacht racing. He must learn also, how to determine when his boat is right and going well; he must have confidence, timing and judgment. This takes time and comes only with experience. There comes a time when correct decisions are made almost instinctively. Although proper preparation beforehand and concentration during the race is still necessary, it ceases eventually to be work and becomes instead a fascinating part of the sport.

The right frame of mind is a prerequisite to winning. Skipper and crew must have a competitive spirit, must want to win and must feel that they have a chance to win. Not that winning is an end in itself. Mug hunting is a poor excuse for racing. But it is more fun to enter a race with the hope of winning and greater satisfaction to look back after it is over and realize that you haven't let your boat down.

But if you don't enjoy a race unless you have won it, it is time to take stock. It is one thing to enjoy winning or at least putting up a stiff fight and quite another if your day is ruined if you don't win. In keen competition, one is apt to win only a small percentage of the races, yet racing is most fun under such circumstances.

We have entitled this book *Sailing to Win*. In one respect, the title is misleading. While the immediate object is to win, the more basic one is to enjoy the sport. Although racing cannot be studied too carefully, it can be taken too seriously. Winning at any cost is certainly no fun at all. Sea lawyers and those who win through unfair advantage are on the wrong tack.

I still remember a race I won over twenty years ago but which I would rather have forgotten. Near the end of the race we were on the port tack crossing the bow of the second boat which was on the starboard tack. Just before we were to cross, the wind headed us and let the other boat up. There was no time to tack, so we skinned across her bow with little to spare. The skipper of the other boat shouted that he would have hit us if he hadn't borne off. My crew backed up my belief that in spite of the wind shift we still would have crossed even if he had held his course. Therefore, we did not drop out and went on to win. The other skipper didn't protest but he plainly felt that he had been fouled. More than twenty years later, I'm still of the opinion that we did not foul him, *but I'm not sure*. One thing is certain—it wasn't worth winning under such doubtful conditions and I've wished many times since that we had dropped out, even though we felt we were within our rights.

Win or lose, the more one studies yacht racing, the more one races and the more one learns about it, the firmer grows the conviction that it is the finest sport on earth.